LINE
DANCING

Maggy Halliday

LINE

DANCING

Maggy Halliday

TEACH YOURSELF BOOKS

For UK order enquiries: please contact Bookpoint Ltd, 39 Milton Park, Abingdon, Oxon OX14 4TD. Telephone: (44) 01235 400414, Fax: (44) 01235 400454. Lines are open from 9.00 - 6.00, Monday to Saturday, with a 24 hour message answering service. Email address: orders@bookpoint.co.uk

For Usa & Canada order queries: please contact NTC/Contemporary Publishing, 4255 West Touhy Avenue, Lincolnwood, Illinois 60646-1975, USA Telephone: (847) 6795500, Fax: (847) 6792494.

Long renowned as the authoritative source for self-guided learning - with more than 30 million copies sold worldwide - the *Teach Yourself* series includes over 200 titles in the fields of languages, crafts, hobbies, sports, and other leisure activities.

A catalogue entry for this title is available from The British Library.

Library of Congress Catalog Card Number: On file

First published in UK 1998 by Hodder Headline Plc, 338 Euston Road, London, NW1 3BH.

First published in US 1998 by NTC/Contemporary Publishing, 4255 West Touhy Avenue, Lincolnwood (Chicago), Illinois 60646-1975 USA.

The 'Teach Yourself' name and logo are registered trademarks of Hodder & Stoughton Ltd.

Cover photo © Telegraph Colour Library

Typeset by Transet Limited, Coventry, England.
Printed in Great Britain for Hodder & Stoughton Educational, a division of Hodder Headline Plc, 338 Euston Road, London, NW1 3BH.

Impression number   10 9 8 7 6 5 4 3 2
Year   2002 2001 2000 1999 1998

CONTENTS

ACKNOWLEDGEMENTS

Loving thanks to my daughter, Julie, who works alongside me and helps to make line dancing even more special. Thanks also for helping with the dancing charts included in the book.

Thanks to the many choreographers for their contributions to the line dance scene, including: Ruth Elias, Bill Bader, Betty Wilson, Jim Long, Sandy Boulton, Texan Tempros, Ray and Tina Yeoman, Linda Deford, Rodeo Cowboys, Barbara J Mason, Gita Renick, Max Perry, Jo Thompson, Neil Hale, Jim and Martie Ferrazzanno, Jenny Rockett, Rodeo Ruth, Michelle Perron, Helen O'Malley.

Thanks also to the patient people who tested out the learning programmes: Alan and Madeline Jenkinson, Fred and Madge Keating, and June Wallwork.

INTRODUCTION

Welcome friend

You have taken your first courageous step towards becoming a line dancer. Be warned, once you have mastered the dances and started to mix with other line dancers, once you have experienced the warm, friendly atmosphere and moved to the rhythmic strains of a live country and western band, **you're hooked**.

This book could possibly change your whole way of life.

The book has been set out clearly and carefully to take you, step by step, through the early stages of line dancing. It is designed for a beginner but the more experienced dancer may also learn from its pages.

Teach Yourself Line Dancing has been organised into five chapters to make it more accessible to you, the reader and would-be dancer.

All about line dancing is designed to give the reader a glimpse into the background of line dance. It describes the recent popularity explosion and gives some ideas as to the reasons for this. With 'tongue in cheek' it moves back through the history of line dancing and on to discussing some recent changes.

Getting Started explains how to get the most value from the charts. It helps you to interpret the musical counts and then organises a learning pattern for you to follow. This learning pattern gives you practice by taking you through one dance step by step. Now you can really get started with your own dancing.

Out and About helps you to find where sessions are held and to decide which to choose. It gives some ideas about what to wear both at your first session and as you progress. It also gives advice on how to act, describing line dance etiquette, procedures and common practices.

Developing Style helps you to bring your own style to line dancing. Ways to improve technique are described and the use of variations to bring individuality into your dancing is encouraged.

Dance Charts help by charting more of the popular dances in order of their difficulty. You will be well and truly hooked by now and anxious to add to your repertoire. Remember to use your learning pattern to master them well. The chapter also tries to wean you towards the more conventional scripts which will not contain foot patterns. Time for these later, though. Use the glossary for fuller descriptions of terms, foot patterns and commonly used figures.

The last part of the book contains information which will prove useful both now and in the future. There is a glossary of line dance terms and figures, a pictorial description of the foot patterns used in the dance charts, a list of the dances contained in the book with details of music suggestions, and a list of useful addresses.

Wishing you the very best of luck with your dancing.

Remember to keep smiling. Line dancing is great fun.

1 | ALL ABOUT LINE DANCING

Line dance fever!

Can there be anyone on this planet who has not heard, or seen, line dancing? I think not. It is certainly experiencing a popularity explosion.

Recently we have been asked to organise line dancing in dance schools, large ballrooms, social clubs, school halls, church halls and community centres. We have danced with the under-12s at 'after school clubs' and the over-80s at 'afternoon tea dances'. We have 'lined' up families at birthday parties, anniversaries and wedding receptions and have been advertised as an alternative method of keeping fit at health centres and night schools. Social secretaries have booked us for their sports clubs, prize-giving events and society get-togethers and I've lost count of the number of fund-raising events we have taken part in. Just last week I was judging a family line dance competition where the youngest competitor was only five years old and the oldest was a very young great grandma of 83. No wonder everyone is anxious to get in on the act.

Whether you go alone or with friends or family, everyone can, and does, dance next to everyone else whatever their age, income group, sexual orientation or ability. Whole families, all ages and communities are brought together on the dance floor.

Between heats at a line dance Championship I was sitting with a small group at the side of the dance floor. They were discussing what they, personally, liked best about line dancing.

Joe and Maddie both have very stressful jobs. 'Trying to keep our minds on the steps as we dance leaves no time for thinking about less positive things that may have happened at work,' they said. In this way, line dancing encourages them to think positively. 'Gradually, over the session,' they said, 'the stresses of our everyday life slowly begin to melt away'. They said they were both making a physical effort to develop their ability to smile and relax and found this was spreading over the rest of their lives.

Bill and Mary have only just started line dancing but have always been social dancers. We all laughed at their reminiscences of the past. There were tales from Bill of searching for friends to go to dances with, then sitting around the bar trying to build up enough courage to actually ask someone to dance. Mary told us how she used to hang around the ballroom like a 'spare part' waiting to be asked. 'It was almost the last dance before the sexes got together and danced,' they recalled. They both said they loved the casual friendliness of the line dance session. 'Everywhere you look,' they laughed, 'people are making mistakes. It just doesn't matter at all. They just start again along with the rest'. They both found this a real comfort and said they never felt embarrassed.

Josie admitted she was a fitness fanatic. 'I was on a low impact aerobics programme,' she said, 'but I find line dancing is just as good a form of exercise'. She explained how she used it to raise her heart rate and build up her stamina and felt it was as safe and easy as any kind of exercise used correctly. 'It means you can exercise in a wonderfully social atmosphere,' she added.

Tony admitted he wasn't a dancer at all but his wife, Lily, was. He said he still felt very welcome in the line dance session. 'I just chat with friends, listen to the music and watch while Lily joins the rest and gets on with the dancing.' 'This suits us fine,' said Lily. 'I'm hoping because Tony doesn't feel threatened in any way, he will eventually end up joining in.'

This was just a small group but their experiences match those of so many others on the line dance scene. Line dancing has many different advantages. Is it surprising it is so popular?

Back down the 'line' – a brief history of line dancing

Billy Ray Cyrus had a lot to answer for in 1993 as he sang about his 'Achy Breaky Heart'. Who could have thought the dance packaged along with the song would take hold as it did, bringing with it a turning point in the popularity of line dancing?

The arena had probably been set 13 years before when John Travolta, with the film *Urban Cowboy*, had lassoed the fashion, music and dance industries and, with the media firmly riding along behind him, reacquainted them with the country and western styles.

Just two years earlier in the movie *Saturday Night Fever*, John had already rocketed dancing as a pastime into the popularity charts as he set the world alight with his routines to 'Disco Inferno' and 'Stayin' Alive'. Queues outside halls and classes to learn the new style of solo line dancing actually equalled those Elvis Presley had attracted when he had 'rocked around the clock' in the 1950s.

There were many line dances to be seen in the 1970s including 'The Hustle' and 'Bus Stop'. These were all being danced to the popular music of the time, including country and western and the 'big band' sound.

The big band sound had been growing in popularity since the 1930s and many dances like Lindy Hop, Big Apple, and The Frug, were part of the dance scene. Some of these were danced in pairs but others were danced solo and in lines.

At the beginning of the twentieth century the Charleston, Black Bottom and the Shimmy were all the rage. Again these were sometimes danced with a partner but just as often danced individually and in lines.

Perhaps the biggest appeal of line dancing stems from our growing interest in the simple way of life. Although line dancing has become an art form it still encourages the close family group. It represents America's frontier past. The early settlers were rugged individuals. They built homes, schools and livelihoods with their bare hands. They worked to give their families a better life. Their families were very important to them. These early settlers, at the end of a hard day of work, would come together to 'let their hair down'. They came from many places around the world and, at first, they would dance the dances of their homeland, the reels from Ireland, the clog dances from England, and so on. From this melting pot would emerge different types of dances, ones which were similar to the originals but no longer identical. Probably the most popular of these was the Jig, similar, and yet different, from its Irish counterpart. In this dance, feet were 'dug', 'kicked', 'scuffed', 'slid' and 'stomped', hips 'thrust' and 'rolled' in exactly the same way we see in dances today, such as 'Tush Push' by Jim Ferrazzano, 'Grundy Gallop' by Jenny Rockett, and 'The Billy'.

Since prehistoric times people have used music and dance to communicate and express themselves. Dance has not only been enjoyed as an art form but as a way to feel good both physically, spiritually and mentally. Through it people have learned to develop self-esteem in their own communal settings. In this way history and culture have been passed down through the ages. Line dancing, like all other dance forms, reflects the history and culture of its source, moulded together by the feelings and attitudes of the present day.

Current changes

There have been many changes in the line dance scene over the past few years. Perhaps the most important change is the way it is perceived. So much has it grown in status that it is now considered an art form in its own right with its own definite terminology, professional bodies and organisations.

Another change is in the style of music used at line dance sessions. Even before line dancing's great boost in popularity, country and western music was attached to it, or the other way around. This is still the case in the main. Many of the older dances such as 'California Freeze' and 'Cowgirl Twist' by Bill Bader are still very popular and are danced to country and western music. There are also many newer dances with choreographers coming from all around the world to join them, like 'Black Coffee' by Helen O'Malley, 'Stroll Along Cha Cha' from Rodeo Cowboys, and 'Wrangler Butts' by Rodeo Ruth. These are also danced to country and western music. However, other music is also being used. One of Elvis's hits from the 1950s, 'All Shook Up', with a dance prepared by Hilary Kershaw, is often seen. There are others, too, which take us back to the past. Some are reminiscent of those dances in the 'big band' era of the 1930s, such as 'Be-Bop-A-Lula' from Denny Hengen and 'Honky Tonk Twist ll' from Max Perry. Others are danced to Irish tunes, for example, 'Tropicana Parking Lot' by Patrick W Riley which is usually danced to 'Lord of the Dance' and 'Electric Reel' by Robert and Regina Padden which is often danced to 'Cry of the Celts'. There are many other examples like this and not everyone welcomes them. Some think line dancing should only be danced to country and western music, while others encourage the inclusion of different rhythms.

Yet another change is the speed at which newer dances are spreading and the wider areas they now reach. This is probably due to the great number of dance magazines, television and radio programmes and touring artists which have grown so much in number.

One thing that has not changed is the friendliness, warmness and wonderful community feeling which prevails, and has always prevailed, at the line dance session.

Isn't it time *you* got into line?

2 | GETTING STARTED

Everyone has to start at the beginning. Dancing comes easy to some people but not to others. Most people start the same way you are going to. They start from the very beginning – and they practise, and then practise some more.

So here goes

How to read the charts

You will be eager to get started on the dances, but pause a minute to understand the layout of the charts and symbols. The information is given in a fairly obvious way but one or two points may need some explanation. Remember, the charts are your vital key. Learn to use them correctly and you will get maximum benefit with minimum effort. The whole layout is explained from the top of the chart through to the end. As you read the explanation it may help to have an actual dance chart in front of you.

The dance title

In all cases this will be at the top of the script. Sometimes the same dance is known by different names in different areas. Where these variations are known, they have also been given.

One, two or four wall dance

This will be the next information seen on each script. It describes the number of different walls you return to at the end of each dance sequence. You may turn many times within the sequence but this is not taken into account here.

Counts

These are placed next to the information about how many walls the dance uses. It describes the number of counts of music which each sequence of the dance will use. It does not describe the number of steps taken. Sometimes, for example, three steps are danced on two counts of music.

Music suggestion

Some dances have actually been written to be danced to a certain piece of music. In this case the dance will best fit that music and the title of this has been given. In other cases, the suggestion is just an indication of the type of music that the dance appears to fit well. To make this easier for the beginner, the majority of our suggestions have been taken from three CDs, details of which can be found at the back of this book. A voucher for these is also included. Each line dance instructor will have their own particular taste in music and will decide which music will be used with this in mind. You could dance one particular dance to a piece of music on one night and then a completely different piece of music on the next occasion. This adds to the fun. Different music helps to give a dance a completely different character.

Choreographer

This is the person who invented the dance, and the names have been included where known.

Memory jogger

This section of the chart will become useful after the dance has been learnt. It is meant to remind you of the dance organisation or to *jog your memory*. Any parts that have been forgotten can easily be found by looking back to the fuller description given in the chart. Each of the lines of the memory jogger represent a section of the dance. These lines have also been printed at the top of the section to which they belong.

Side headings

The separate sections that have been written in the memory jogger have been broken down into smaller pieces. These have been placed, in bold print, in the left-hand column, next to their descriptions.

Direction

The direction in which the figure moves is printed under its name. It is always inside brackets and written in italics, for example, *(moving L)*.

Foot descriptions

These are given in both written and pictorial form. There are two reasons for this. At first, the beginner may get the most understanding from the pictorial form. As the figures become known, the written form will become much easier. The beginner, it is hoped, will be slowly weaned over to this written form. It is important for this to happen as charts are more commonly written in this form.

The solid footprints indicate which foot your weight will be on at the end of each count.

Counts

At the bottom of each block the count number is written in bold italics, for example, *count 1*. This describes the count of music on which each step is taken. Normally there will be one step taken for each count of music. This is not always the case, though. In shuffles, for example, there are three steps taken on only two counts of music. The *&* count is then used, i.e. three steps – *counts 1 & 2*.

Notes

If there are any commonly known regional versions to the dance then these are given. If none is given, this does not necessarily mean that they do not exist – just that they are not common. The regional variations give flavour to the line dance scene. They add yet another element of fun. Don't look on these versions as being 'incorrect'. In America, many of the States deliberately set out to put their own slight differences to a popular dance. This means many different versions arrive in different parts of the world. Do remember, though, it is good manners always to dance the version being danced at that particular club. Never attempt to impose your own version.

What about the music?

Line dancing and music go hand in hand

The music will actually help with the dancing and certainly makes it more enjoyable. Spend some time just listening to the music you are going to dance to. Try tapping out its rhythm. This will be time well spent. the dance sequences are separated into counts of music with the steps matching them. The beats will signal when to move.

4/4 time

All the dances in this book are in 4/4 time, except for State Line Waltz. This means there are four counts in each bar. If you listen to the music suggested for Tennessee Stroll you should be able to pick out the four counts easily. Try counting out 1, 2, 3, 4, 1, 2, 3, 4 while the music is playing. The first count in each bar is the accentuated one. The singer will usually emphasise the first count of the bar so this should confirm whether your counting is correct.

3/4 time

The State Line Waltz, along with all modern waltzes, is played in 3/4 time. All the above will still apply but this time with three counts to the bar. You will need to try counting these while the Waltz music is being played. Again, the emphasised count is the first one.

When to begin the dance

You usually begin to dance just after the singing starts. Try starting the music a number of times until you are quite confident of both the count and where you will begin to dance.

Choose your own music

Although we have suggested music for each of the dances in the book, please do not feel limited by these. If you are careful about the rhythm of each dance you will be able to enjoy putting the dances to different music.

Setting up a learning programme

The *way* in which you learn any dance will determine how long you will be able to remember it. It helps by building up a definite learning routine.

The learning routine we are using is the 'RUDA' method. It is built on sound learning principles and I think you will find it very effective.

RUDA is short for *Relax, Understand, Dance and Accumulate*.

Relax

Play the suggested music for the dance, or a similar piece you have chosen. Tap out the rhythm with your feet. Pick out where you will start to dance. Be aware of the build-up to this. Now you know the speed at which the dance will move and just where to begin.

You will be able to concentrate far better on your learning if you are free from stress. Make a point of deliberately relaxing your shoulders and breathing deeply. Smiling also helps you to relax.

Understand

Look at the whole chart as it stands. Don't think about dancing it yet. Just make sure you understand the layout. If you are unsure about anything, turn again to the section which explains how to read the charts. Study both the written and the pictorial descriptions until you are sure you know what it is asking you to do.

Dance

- When you are confident you know what the chart is asking you to do, 'walk' through the block of steps to be learnt using the written and pictorial instructions to help you.
- Perform the dance saying the steps as you move, for example, - **side, behind, side, tap**.
- Perform the dance saying the counts as you move, for example, **1, 2, 3, 4**.
- Perform the dance to the music from memory. Dance until you are confident.

Accumulate

Add the block just learnt to the sections already learnt. Continue until you can dance the whole dance so far, confidently, to music.

Practice sessions

The timing of your practice sessions is also important. Aim to practise regularly, when you are unlikely to be disturbed. That way you can concentrate totally on the session. Practising regularly also helps you to build previous learning before it is forgotten.

Tips

- Allow yourself one main learning session of approximately one hour. Try to practise regularly.
- When you are confident with what you have been learning, have a ten-minute break.
- Now spend another ten minutes going through the complete 'RUDA' programme again to revise your learning.
- At your next session spend five minutes revising your previous learning, again using the complete 'RUDA' programme.
- Each time you take on another main section of learning, do a quick revision of the dances already learnt. This will serve to keep them in your memory.

You are now ready to begin dancing the Tennessee Stroll

Practice dance

Tennessee Stroll

One wall dance. 16 counts
Music suggestion: 'Me & My Baby' (130bpm)
Choreographer: Unknown

Memory jogger

Counts 1–8: Vine L, brush. Vine R, brush.
Counts 9–16: Side, brush, side, dig, kick, dig, kick, stomp-up.

Description with foot patterns

Counts 1 – 8: Vine L, brush. Vine R, brush

Vine L *(moving L)*	Step L foot to side.	Step R foot behind L foot.	Step L foot to side.	Brush R foot next to L foot.
	Count 1	Count 2	Count 3	Count 4
Vine R *(moving R)*	Step R foot to side.	Step L foot behind R foot.	Step R foot to side.	Brush L foot next to R foot.
	Count 5	Count 6	Count 7	Count 8

Counts: 9 – 16: Side, brush, side, dig, kick, dig, kick, stomp-up

Side, brush, *(moving L)* **side, dig** *(moving R)*	Step L foot to side.	Brush R foot next to L foot.	Step R foot to side.	Dig L heel forward.
	Count 9	Count 10	Count 11	Count 12
Kick, dig, kick, stomp-up *(on the spot)*	Kick L foot forward.	Dig L heel forward.	Kick L foot forward.	Stomp L foot next to R foot without weight.
	Count 13	Count 14	Count 15	Count 16

Begin again.

Learning to dance the Tennessee Stroll

Now to start the learning programme proper. Check the definitions in the Glossary if you are uncertain about any of the terms. As explained previously, we are using the RUDA learning method.

The first block – counts 1–8
Relax

Play the music suggested for the dance, 'Me & My Baby', or a similar piece which you have chosen. Pick out the rhythm.

Relax your shoulders, breathe deeply and smile.

Understand

Carefully look through the first block on the dance chart. Look up anything you do not understand. Study the written and pictorial descriptions on the chart. Don't move on until you understand exactly what it is asking you to do.

Dance

- 'Walk' through the first block of steps to be learnt, using the written and pictorial instructions to help you.
- Perform the block saying the steps as you move, i.e. - side, behind, side, brush, side, behind, side, brush.
- Perform the block saying the counts as you move, i.e. 1, 2, 3, 4, 5, 6, 7, 8.
- Perform the dance to the music. Dance until you are confident with what you have learnt.

Accumulate

As you are only on the first block there is nothing, yet, to accumulate.

The second block – counts 9–16
Relax

Again, play the music suggested for the dance. Pick out the rhythm.

Relax your shoulders, breathe deeply and smile.

Understand

Look closely at the instructions for the second block on the dance chart. Study again the written and pictorial descriptions on the chart.

Dance

- 'Walk' through the second block of steps using the written and pictorial instructions to help you.

- Perform the block saying the steps as you move, i.e. side, brush, side, dig, kick, dig, kick, stomp-up. (Remember a stomp-up means you will use this foot again for the next movement.)
- Perform the block saying the counts as you move, i.e. 9, 10, 11, 12, 13, 14, 15, 16.
- Perform the block to the music from memory until you are confident.

Accumulate

Using the whole RUDA programme, dance through the two blocks together until you are confident with what you have learnt.

Congratulations! Wasn't that easy? You have now learnt Tennessee Stroll. Now try a few more dances from level one. Good luck. Remember to use the RUDA learning programme and the timing schedule whenever you set out to learn another line dance.

3 | OUT AND ABOUT

When and where?

Line dancing is a 'together' event. It is much more fun in company and is so popular it is now possible to find instruction sessions most mornings, afternoons and evenings. Just think through your weekly timetable, decide which days and times of the day would be most suitable for you, then fill in Table 3.1 'When can I go line dancing?'. Put a tick against the sessions where a line dance class would fit in comfortably with your own schedule.

Table 3.1 When can I go line dancing?

	9–11 a.m.	11a.m.– 1p.m.	1–3 p.m.	3-5 p.m.	5–7 p.m.	7–9 p.m.	9–11 p.m.
Monday							
Tuesday							
Wednesday							
Thursday							
Friday							
Saturday							
Sunday							

Finding where to go is fairly easy.

■ **Get a copy of a line dance magazine**. If you haven't started taking any of the line dance magazines then send for a copy. You will find them in the 'Useful Addresses' section. Most are really interesting and they usually have a list of line dance sessions or telephone numbers in the back.

- **Ring up any of the dance organisations**. They are usually very helpful. Some addresses are also at the end of this book.

- **Take a look through your local newspaper and free editions.** Many dance organisers advertise, especially in the 'What's on' sections.

- **Ring up your local evening institutes, health studios, clubs and public houses**. Many run line dance sessions, or know where they are being run.

- **Speak to all your friends, colleagues and friends of friends.** Many will go to line dancing themselves, or at least know someone who does. Carefully write down all your findings in Table 3.2 'Where can I go line dancing?'. At first you will be looking for classes for beginners, but think of your future programme as well. Make a note of all the line dance sessions in your area then put a ring around the ones which fit in with your own schedule best.

Place	Day	Time	Cost	Level	Qualified Instructor ✓ ✗

Table 3.2 Where can I go line dancing?

Evaluating the sessions

As you try the different line dance sessions you will find that some suit you more than others. Tables 3.3 and 3.4 will help you to record your impressions of each session visited, enabling you to make a confident decision about which session will suit you best.

Here are some suggestions for assessing sessions:

Deciding which session to attend

The type of session which suits you best will largely depend on the type of person you are. Each session will be slightly different. Some people learn best in an academic type place, others in a club atmosphere. Sessions for beginners are held in many different kinds of places. You need to compare and contrast a few completely different types of sessions before you make any decisions. Do try to make at least one of them a country and western club if this is possible. They can be quite an experience.

Access

If the session is within easy walking distance for you, give it a high rating in the chart (see Table 3.4). If it is not, travelling time will need to be taken into consideration. Parking spaces become a factor if you need to take a car. You need also to ask yourself if the area in which the session is being held is a safe one at the time you will be visiting it.

Atmosphere

On your first visit to any session you will know whether you would like to become a regular visitor there. Friendliness plays an important part in line dancing. Some sessions instantly feel warm, friendly and welcoming. These are the places you are looking for and to which you can give a high rating.

Instruction

If the instructor has a welcoming personality this will affect the whole atmosphere of the session. Learning will be easier and far more fun. A good instructor will:

- have a clear voice which holds everybody's attention
- break down and build up a dance using suitably sized learning sections
- use the correct names for figures being taught, thereby building up the class vocabulary
- 'listen' to the class, making learning a two-way process
- give thought to their appearance and the role they are playing.

A higher rating may be given for the instructor who scores well on all, or most of, the above points.

Music

Music plays an important part at a line dance session but everyone's taste may be slightly different. Some general considerations may be whether:

- ■ your taste and that of the instructor are compatible
- ■ the tone is easy on the ear
- ■ the sound is correct, neither too loud nor to soft
- ■ the equipment is suitable.

If the music enhances the night for you, then a high rating is deserved.

Session number	Name of session visited	Address	Telephone number
(example)	CW Texan Line	63 Chicago Road, Illinois, USA	06443 348962
1			
2			
3			
4			
5			
6			

Table 3.3 Sessions visited

After each session look at Table 3.4 'Which session will suit me best?' Follow the column for the session you have just attended and give it a score out of ten in each of the five categories: type of session, ease of access, atmosphere, instruction/instructor and music. Then add up all the scores. When you have attended each of the trial sessions, the Table should help you decide which would suit you best.

Session attended	(example)	1	2	3	4	5	6
Type of session	8						
Ease of access	7						
Atmosphere	9						
Instruction/Instructor	9						
Music	7						
Total	40						

Table 3.4 Which session will suit me best?

First-hand experiences

Three would-be line dancers who have just completed their trial session write about their experiences.

Jane, who worked full-time, said she was pleasantly surprised by how much she had enjoyed her first session which had been at the local evening institute. 'Many of the folks were absolute beginners,' she said 'I felt quite experienced.' She thought the instructions had been a bit laboured and the instructor's choice of music had left her cold. She had filled in Table 3.4 accordingly. Her second session had been her favourite. It was at one of the local health clubs. The instruction was clear and although the instructor did not use many different discs, those used were OK. 'I loved the atmosphere,' she said. 'Of course, I've always liked the health club scene.' This one got the highest score on the table.

Bob, who is self-employed, absolutely adored the country and western clubs. 'I had never experienced anything like them,' he said. 'They were quite something.' He loved the instructions and managed the dances well. The parking was also very good. One of the clubs was easier to get to than the other so the mark-up on the chart was higher. He decided to visit this club regularly. He marked one of the clubs near to home quite high too and said he was going to continue to go there also.

Louise, a young mother, gave the local institute session quite high marks but two of the clubs had scored higher because they were so handy. They also fitted perfectly into her own timetable. She decided to visit both of them regularly. 'Obviously, I scored some of the instructors higher than others,' Louise said thoughtfully, 'but the two clubs I have chosen scored equally well in total and the atmosphere at both has to be experienced to be believed.' She said she had already made many friends.

What shall I wear?

You have, no doubt, seen line dancers either on the television or on the front of videos or CDs. They are probably wearing tasselled outfits and huge buckled belts. They invariably have knee-length boots and cowboy hats. Do you need to invest in clothes like this before attending your first session? People's opinion about Western gear varies. Some like it, some don't. But no one likes to look out of place. It is true, the smell of the leather does play a bit part in creating the wonderful rich atmosphere of a line dancing evening, but this does not mean you need to dash out and buy a full outfit.

Dress casually at your first line dance session

Even in the most 'way out' country and western dance clubs, where the most outlandish outfits are seen, there will still be many people who are wearing very simple, casual clothing. These people will never look out of place. If the first sessions you attend are at the local community centre or night school then casual clothing will be the norm. When you go to your first few sessions you will probably feel far more at ease if you go in for the more casual look. Here are some guidelines towards the kind of clothes to choose for a visit to a line dance session, regardless of where this might be.

Choose casual, comfortable clothing

Line dancing involves a great deal of twisting and turning. It requires the dancer to have unrestricted use of the legs for swings, hitches and turns and of the arms and body for claps, shimmies, etc. This calls for clothes which are loose fitting and hardwearing and which do not present any restrictions. Under this category you may include T-shirts, plain or checked open-neck shirts with either short or loose-fitting sleeves, jeans, corduroy trousers or loose-styled skirts.

Footwear

The feet play a considerable part in line dancing. A variety of foot movements are involved, many of which could lead to injury without the proper footwear. Footwear needs to be firm, sturdy and low heeled. Try to avoid sandals or high heels because these do not give the foot the necessary support. The height of the heel can cause the whole body balance to become disturbed, leading to quite severe problems. Wearing the wrong type of footwear can cause all kinds of aches, pains and tensions in the body.

There are numerous kinds of foot swivels involved in line dancing. Soles need to be smooth enough to accommodate these. For example, the sole of the trainer grips the floor, making ankle damage a possibility.

You are now suitably attired for your first communal line dance session. Good luck.

Dressing more adventurously

When you have been dancing for a while and are feeling more confident, you may like to be a bit more adventurous.

Boots

These will need a great deal of consideration. Even in the middle of winter line dancing is hot work. A basic pair of leather boots will probably cost more than the most elaborate plastic ones, but are far better value. They will leave your feet just as cool and comfortable at the end of the night as they were at the beginning. There are many items you may use to brighten up your boots, such as chains, feathers and studs. All these can be bought quite cheaply and attached easily.

The hat

Hats with plastic linings tend to be the cheapest but perhaps not the best. A great deal of body heat is lost through the top of the head, which causes the plastic lining and the hair to become damp. This can become unpleasant as the night progresses. Felt hats are dearer but cooler and when decorated with chains and feathers can look very smart.

Belts

Belts make a huge difference to an outfit. They are usually broad and again, for comfort, in leather. A plastic belt will cause you to perspire and feel very uncomfortable by the end of the night. There are a variety of highly decorated buckles on the market which the stall or shop owner will usually fix for you.

Outfits

There are a great deal of different outfits you can try. All these can be bought from any western shop or stall which are listed in the line dance magazines. Many have tassels and are often in leather or suede. When you have visited a western shop and have some idea of the styles worn, you may feel able to make your own outfits. Dancers often do. If you want to be really adventurous, you may like to get a long black duster coat or sheriff's outfit, or even an Indian outfit complete with beads and head-dress. The choice is yours.

Extras

There are many extras that can be bought to smarten up an outfit. You will find studs in most markets, which can be fitted on to an existing waistcoat, shirt or pair of trousers. Clip-on collar tips can be bought quite cheaply, along with arm bands, bolos (a thin leather strap with a metal motif) and boot straps. A browse around any country and western stall is always interesting.

Rules of etiquette

Line dance etiquette is mainly a matter of common sense but there are a few rules of which you need to be aware.

Although line dancing is easy, the floor is often very crowded so dancers occasionally bump into other participants. When this happens, just smile, apologise and carry on. Dancers need to consider each other or enjoyment could be lost.

General rules

- Always walk around the outside of the dance floor, especially during a dance.

- Try not to sit in someone else's place.
- Leave your cans, drinks, glasses and food off the floor when dancing.
- If you smoke, remember to put out your cigarette before moving on to the floor.
- Move off the floor to chat or help anyone with a dance.
- Always remember to keep your head up.
- Arms and hands should be out of the way unless they are needed for a clap or a slap. Hands may be held behind the back, placed in front on the belt or hooked in the front pockets. This applies even when dancing spins or turns.
- Dancers should try to leave enough space to move in each direction. If the floor is crowded, they will need to take smaller steps and try to avoid any collisions. Please remember to apologise right away if bumps do occur, whether it is your fault or not.

Personal hygiene

There can be very large numbers of people at Western Dance sessions, all using a great deal of energy. Everyone tends to get a bit hot and sticky by the end of the night, so it is important to pay very special attention to personal hygiene.

Teaching sessions

Beginner's sessions

Never add your own variations to dances during beginner's sessions. Leave these until the more advanced sessions. Absolute beginners, especially, watch their fellow dancers and are easily put off by people changing the basic structure of a dance. Always try to be helpful. Remember others could be feeling even more vulnerable than you do yourself.

Intermediate/advanced sessions

Always try to use the dance variation taught, or danced, at that particular venue.

Free dancing

If the DJ announces a particular dance

When the DJ has announced a dance, *only* this dance should be performed. It is considered extremely bad manners to start another dance under these circumstances.

When no particular dance has been announced

Sometimes the DJ, or band, will announce the music they are playing rather than a set dance. This usually means the dancers may choose their own dance. Obviously, much greater awareness is then needed by the dancers because there may be more than one dance on the floor at the same time.

You may:

- join a line dance already started. If someone has started a dance which you know, feel free to join them. Line dancers use the centre of the room, leaving the outside rings for partner dancers. Always start another line rather than join one that is likely to block the outside rings. The partner dancers always have right of way.

- start a line dance of your own choice. If you wish to start a dance of your own choice, first consider whether it is suitable for other dancers at that particular session. If it is, then go to the front of the dance floor so that others can fall in line behind you. Only start a different dance if there is plenty of room on the dance floor.

- start or join, a partner dance. Remember always to ask someone to partner you in a courteous manner. It is usual to ask someone near to you. If they refuse then accept this as nicely as possible. If you have refused to dance with someone, it is considered very bad manners to accept someone else.

Partner dances

The partner dancers move around the outside of the dance floor. The fast-moving partner dancers will move around in an outer ring. The slower-moving partner dancers will move in an inner ring.

■ The centre of the dance floor is often used for partner dances which are fairly stationary. Many of the line dances can also be done with a partner and these are danced in the centre part of the dance floor. Of course, line dancers will also be dancing in this part. Always be aware of partner dancers who are moving around the dance floor.

■ The inner ring is for stop-and-go partner dances, such as Swings. The Western Barn Dance falls in this category. They are also danced in an anti- or counter-clockwise direction. Again, always be careful to avoid bumping other dancers on the floor.

■ The outer ring is for continually moving partner dances, such as Two Step or Polka. These always move in an anti- or counter- clockwise direction around the dance floor. Slower dancers should allow faster dancers to pass on the outside of them. Always be extra careful of other dancers on the floor.

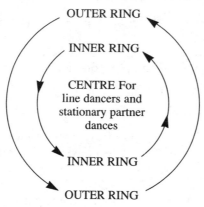

Figure 3.1 Line of dance

In partner dances which move around the dance floor, the 'line of dance' always moves in an anti- or counter- clockwise direction. In some dances, for one or two steps, a clockwise direction is occasionally used. This is usually termed moving 'against line of dance' or 'reverse line of dance'.

4 | DEVELOPING STYLE

When first starting line dancing, movements tend to be rough and jerky. Gradually, muscles grow accustomed to the different kinds of movement and dancing becomes smoother. Soon, learning steps becomes far easier, even the more intricate ones, and it is possible to think more about how to make the dances 'look better'. This can often be achieved by improving technique and adding individual variations to the dances.

Improving technique

The dictionary tells us 'technique' means 'skill or art applied to a practical task'. The practical task here is line dancing. The skill or art can be applied through body awareness, poise, correct use of rise and sway and sympathetic interpretation of the music. In other words, paying attention to the 'way' the dance is performed rather than merely the steps.

Body awareness

Practise moving different parts of the body to music to become more aware of how they move. This includes the way the head and body is held, the body balance, the use of shoulders and feet, etc. This can be done while dancing. First, be very conscious of the head. Move it in different ways as you dance. Choose which way feels 'right' to you. Next progress through the shoulders, chest, hips, and so on. Gradually, you will learn how each body part moves best.

Poise

As you come on to the dance floor, stand in a natural upright position with the knees slightly flexed. Settle the weight of the body evenly over the balls of both feet. Feel some control at the waist but leave shoulders relaxed and chest without tension. When moving forward, keep the body balance forward without pushing the hips out of alignment. The correct posture will give a pleasant feeling of upward and downward stretch in the back, while the shoulders remain relaxed giving a feeling of freedom to every move. When starting a dance, the whole of the weight of the body will be on the ball of the stationary foot. As you walk forward or backward the movement is from the hips rather than the knees. Even movements involving the knee, such as a flick or hitch, will begin at the hips. Knees should be neither too stiff nor too bent. Unless the knees are flexible, movements will be jerky and unpleasant to dance or watch. All parts of the body relate and effect each other.

Rise and sway

Some figures such as the rolling vine, can look really good if the correct type of rise throughout the whole body is used. Rise here is begun by bracing the muscles of the legs, straightening the knees and stretching the body upwards. The rise begins at the end of the first step. At the end of the turn lower by flexing the knees.

Sway can also improve the look of these figures. Sway needs to come right from the ankles and through the whole body. It will help with balance and looks great. When making any turns, sway will be inwards towards the inside of the circle.

The first step of the rolling vine will be straight, use sway on the second step and then straighten again on the third step. Give it a try. Don't attempt to use sway on spins or pivots as balance will be lost.

Musical interpretation

Different types of music require different interpretation. A Waltz will not have the same kind of dance action as a ChaCha or a Swing. Each type of music has it's own rhythmic 'feel'. A Waltz needs to be danced with slow, smooth, deliberate steps, whereas a ChaCha has a 'cheeky' feel. Dancers need to feel the character of the music and let this become a part of the movement.

Adding variations

Many interesting improvisations can be added to line dances with practice. They are perfectly acceptable providing they move the same way as other dancers, take the same length of time as the original steps and leave you on the right foot and in an appropriate position to continue with the original routine. Perhaps you would like to try some of the variations listed below. Do exercise caution as there can be an element of danger, especially if the dance floor is crowded. Do not try them out when there are beginners on the dance floor. It is so easy to take away their self-confidence.

Vine

Many line dances have vines or 'side, close, side' steps in them. Whenever these appear it is possible to dance an 'open turn' or 'rolling vine' instead. The notes for these are in the glossary.

With a great deal of practice a number of spins can be danced instead of one on the same three counts.

Backward and forward walks

Turns can even be substituted for backward and forward walks. They do need to follow the original line of travel and care needs to be taken not to bump into other dancers. Keep feet apart, take smaller steps and try not to become unbalanced or disorientated as you turn.

Step and tap

When dancing a series of 'forward and tap' or 'back and tap' movements, instead dance 'step and slap leather' or 'zig zag' jumps. The zig-zag movement will travel in the same direction as the step and taps.

Pigeon toes

Any line dance which has two pigeon toes leaves itself open to many different variations for the advanced dancer. Jumps can be danced, jump feet apart, crossed, apart, together. Swivets or applejacks are another alternative.

Try some of your own

These kinds of movements bring individuality into line dancing. Be careful not to put in so many substitutes as to virtually make it a different dance and, again, do remember to be careful not to obstruct other dancers.

5 | DANCE CHARTS

Line dances are sequences of steps that form a pattern. These patterns are repeated for the duration of the music.

Line dance patterns range from a few relatively simple steps to very lengthy arrangements of intricate moves. As in anything else, if you are just beginning to learn line dancing you will be more successful if you begin with the easier dances and move on to the more difficult.

The dance descriptions in the book have been arranged in levels, from level 1 to level 7, according to their complexity. Within each category, the dances that appear early are generally made up of fewer, less complicated steps, or are designed to be danced more slowly.

As you will have gathered from your earlier dances, many of the steps or individual foot movements that make up dances are used so frequently and in so many dances that they have special names, for example brush, dig, swing.

You will also be aware that individual steps can often be grouped into combinations or sequences of steps that frequently recur and are used in a variety of dances. These combinations are put together in different ways to form dances. If you can learn to see dances not as sequences of many steps but as patterns of combinations, you will find the dances easier to learn and remember.

Level 1 dance charts

The Freeze

Four wall dance. 16 counts
Music suggestion: A1 Blues
Choreographer: Unknown

Memory jogger

Counts 1–8: Vine R & L with hitches
Counts 9–16: Steps back with a hitch, rocks with a hitch tng ¼ to L

Description with foot patterns
Counts 1–8: Vine R & L with hitches

Vine R with a hitch (moving R)	Step R foot to side.	Step L foot behind R foot.	Step R foot to side.	Hitch L leg.
	Count 1	Count 2	Count 3	Count 4
Vine L with a hitch (moving L)	Step L foot to side.	Step R foot behind L foot.	Step L foot to side.	Hitch R leg.
	Count 5	Count 6	Count 7	Count 8

Counts 9–16: Steps back with a hitch, rocks with a hitch tng ¼ to L

Steps back with a hitch (moving back)	Step R foot back.	Step L foot back.	Step R foot back.	Hitch L leg.
	Count 9	Count 10	Count 11	Count 12

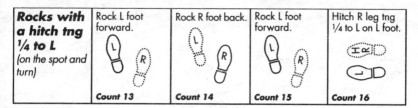

Rocks with a hitch tng ¼ to L (on the spot and turn)	Rock L foot forward.	Rock R foot back.	Rock L foot forward.	Hitch R leg tng ¼ to L on L foot.
	Count 13	Count 14	Count 15	Count 16

Begin again.

Fuzzy Duck Slide

Four wall dance. 16 counts
Music suggestion: Stetson Hat
Choreographer: Unknown

Memory jogger

Counts 1–8: Point R side and close twice, point L side and close twice
Counts 9–16: Touch forward and close twice, step, close, side, slide

Description with foot patterns

Counts 1–8: Point R side and close twice, point L side and close twice

Point R side and close twice (on the spot)	Point R toe to side.	Close R foot to L foot without weight.	Point R toe to side.	Close R foot to L foot.
	Count 1	Count 2	Count 3	Count 4
Point L side and close twice (on the spot)	Point L toe to side.	Close L foot to R foot without weight.	Point L toe to side.	Close L foot to R foot.
	Count 5	Count 6	Count 7	Count 8

Counts 9–16: Point forward and close twice, step, close, side, slide

Point forward and close twice (on the spot)	Point R toe forward.	Close R foot to L foot without weight.	Point R toe forward.	Close R foot to L foot without weight.
	Count 9	Count 10	Count 11	Count 12
Step and close, side, slide (tng R then moving L)	Step R foot forward ¼ to R.	Close L foot to R foot without any weight.	Step L foot to side.	Slide R foot to L foot without weight.
	Count 13	Count 14	Count 15	Count 16

Begin again.

Grapevine Swing

Four wall dance. 18 counts
Music suggestion: Heartbeat
Choreographer: Unknown

Memory jogger

Counts 1–8: Vine R & L
Counts 9–18: Side, close, 3 forward and hitch tng L, 3 back and kick

Description with foot patterns
Counts 1–8: Vine R & L

Vine R (moving R)	Step R foot to side.	Step L foot behind R foot.	Step R foot to side.	Kick L foot across R leg.
	Count 1	Count 2	Count 3	Count 4

Vine L (moving L)	Step L foot to side.	Step R foot behind L foot.	Step L foot to side.	Kick R foot across L leg.
	Count 5	Count 6	Count 7	Count 8

Counts 9–18: Side, close, 3 forward and hitch tng L, 3 back and kick

Side, close (moving R)	Step R foot to side.	Close L foot to R foot.		
	Count 9	Count 10		
3 forward, hitch and turn (moving forward then tng L)	Step R foot forward.	Step L foot forward.	Step R foot forward.	Hitch L leg tng ¼ to L.
	Count 11	Count 12	Count 13	Count 14
3 Back and kick (moving back)	Step L foot back.	Step R foot back.	Step L foot back.	Kick R leg across L leg.
	Count 15	Count 16	Count 17	Count 18

Begin again.

Kensas City Stomp

Four wall dance. 20 counts
Music suggestion: Dancing Boots
Choreographer: Unknown

Memory jogger

Counts 1–4: Forward, slide, step, stomp
Counts 5–12: Vine R, stomp twice, vine L tng, close
Counts 13–20: Step, kick, 3 steps back, 3 stomps

Description with foot patterns
Counts 1–4: Forward, slide, step, stomp

Forward, slide, step, stomp (moving forward)	Step L foot forward.	Slide R foot up to L foot.	Step L foot forward.	Stomp-up R foot next to L foot.
	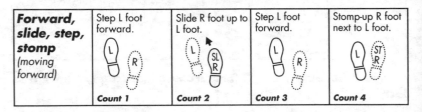 L R	L SL R	L R	L ST R
	Count 1	**Count 2**	**Count 3**	**Count 4**

Counts 5–12: Vine R, stomp twice, vine L tng, close

Vine R and stomp twice (moving R)	Step R foot to side.	Step L foot behind R foot.	Step R foot to side.	Stomp-up L foot next to R foot twice.
	L R	R L	L R	ST L R
	Count 5	**Count 6**	**Count 7**	**Count 8**
Vine L tng, close (moving L)	Step L foot to side.	Step R foot behind L foot.	Step L foot to side tng ¼ to L.	Close R foot to L foot.
	L R	L R	R L	R L
	Count 9	**Count 10**	**Count 11**	**Count 12**

Counts 13–20: Step, kick, 3 steps back, 3 stomps

Step and kick (moving forward)	Step L foot forward.	Kick R foot forward.
	R L	K R L
	Count 13	**Count 14**

3 steps back, 3 stomps (moving back)	Step R foot back.	Step L foot back.	Step R foot back.	Stomp-up L foot next to R foot 3 times.
	Count 15	Count 16	Count 17	Count 18, 19, 20

Begin again.

Alpine

Four wall dance. 28 counts
Music suggestion: Jackknife
Choreographer: Unknown

Memory jogger

Counts 1–8: Fans
Counts 9–16: Heel digs
Counts 17–24: Hooks
Counts 25–28: Vine tng L and stomp

Description with foot patterns

Counts 1–8: Fans

Fans (on the spot)	Keeping heels together, fan R toes out to side.	Close R toes to L toes without weight.	Keeping heels together, fan R toes out to side.	Close R toes to L toes.
	Count 1	Count 2	Count 3	Count 4
	Keeping heels together. Fan L toes out to side.	Close L toes to R toes without weight.	Keeping heels together. Fan L toes out to side.	Close L toes to R toes.
	Count 5	Count 6	Count 7	Count 8

Counts 9–16: Heel digs

Heel digs (on the spot)	Dig R heel forward.	Close R foot to L foot without weight.	Dig R heel forward.	Close R foot to L foot.
	Count 9	Count 10	Count 11	Count 12
	Dig L heel forward.	Close L foot to R foot without weight.	Dig L heel forward.	Close L foot to R foot.
	Count 13	Count 14	Count 15	Count 16

Counts 17–24: Hooks

Hooks (on the spot)	Dig R heel forward.	Hook R heel across L leg	Dig R heel forward.	Close R foot to L foot.
	Count 17	Count 18	Count 19	Count 20
	Dig L heel forward.	Hook L heel across R leg.	Dig L heel forward.	Close L foot to R foot without weight.
	Count 21	Count 22	Count 23	Count 24

Counts 25–28: Vine tng L and stomp

Vine tng L and stomp (moving L and tng L)	Step L foot to side.	Step R foot behind L foot.	Step L foot to side making 1/4 turn to L.	Stomp R foot next to L foot without weight.
	Count 25	Count 26	Count 27	Count 28

Begin again.

Queen of Memphis

Four wall dance. 32 counts
Music suggestion: Queen of Memphis; The Sun Don't Shine on Me
Choreographer: Unknown

Memory jogger

Counts 1–8: Dig, close R twice, dig, close L twice
Counts 9–16: Point forward, side, kick behind and close, R & L
Counts 17–24: Heel struts, R, L, R, L
Counts 25–32: Jazz box tng and jazz box

Description with foot patterns
Counts 1–8: Dig, close R twice, dig, close L twice

Dig, close R *twice* (on the spot)	Dig R heel forward.	Close R foot to L foot without weight.	Dig R heel forward.	Close R foot to L foot.
	Count 1	Count 2	Count 3	Count 4
Dig, close L *twice* (on the spot)	Dig L heel forward.	Close L foot to R foot without weight.	Dig L heel forward.	Close L foot to R foot.
	Count 5	Count 6	Count 7	Count 8

Counts 9–16: Point forward, side, kick behind and close, R & L

Point R *forward,* *side, kick* *behind and* *close* (on the spot)	Point R toe forward.	Point R toe to side.	Kick R foot behind L leg.	Close R foot to L foot.
	Count 9	Count 10	Count 11	Count 12

Point L forward, side, kick behind and close (on the spot)	Point L toe forward.	Point L toe to side.	Kick L foot behind R leg.	Close L foot to R foot.
	Count 13	Count 14	Count 15	Count 16

Counts 17–24: Heel struts, R, L, R, L

Heel struts R & L (moving forward)	Step R heel forward.	Slap R toe down to floor.	Step L heel forward.	Slap L toe down to floor.
	Count 17	Count 18	Count 19	Count 20
Heel struts R & L (moving forward)	Step R heel forward.	Slap R toe down to floor.	Step L heel forward.	Slap L toe down to floor.
	Count 21	Count 22	Count 23	Count 24

Counts 25–32: Jazz box tng and jazz box

Jazz box tng (on the spot then tng R)	Step R across in front of L foot.	Step L foot back.	Step R foot to side tng 1/4 to R.	Close L foot to R foot.
	Count 25	Count 26	Count 27	Count 28
Jazz box (on the spot)	Step R across in front of L foot.	Step L foot back.	Step R foot to side.	Close L foot to R foot.
	Count 29	Count 30	Count 31	Count 32

Begin again.

California Freeze

Four wall dance. 24 counts
Music suggestion: Oh Johnny
Choreographer: Unknown

Memory jogger

Counts 1–8: Vine R & L with hitches
Counts 9–16: Step hitches forward, 3 steps back and hitch
Counts 17–24: Hip bumps and hitch tng L

Description with foot patterns
Counts 1–8: Vine R & L with hitches

Vine R and hitch (moving R)	Step R foot to side.	Step L foot behind R foot.	Step R foot to side.	Hitch L leg.
	Count 1	Count 2	Count 3	Count 4
Vine L and hitch (moving L)	Step L foot to side.	Step R foot behind L foot.	Step L foot to side.	Hitch R leg.
	Count 5	Count 6	Count 7	Count 8

Counts 9–16: Step hitches forward, 3 steps back and hitch

Step, hitch twice (moving forward)	Step R foot forward.	Hitch L leg.	Step L foot forward.	Hitch R leg.
	Count 9	Count 10	Count 11	Count 12
3 steps back, hitch (moving back)	Step R foot back.	Step L foot back.	Step R foot back.	Hitch L leg.
	Count 13	Count 14	Count 15	Count 16

Counts 17–24: Hip bumps and hitch tng L

Hip bumps and hitch tng L	Step L foot forward pushing L hip forward.	Hold foot position pushing L hip forward again.	Hold foot position pushing R hip back.	Hold foot position pushing R hip back again.
	Count 17	Count 18	Count 19	Count 20
	Hold foot position pushing L hip forward.	Hold foot position pushing R hip back.	Hold foot position pushing L hip forward.	Hitch R leg tng ¼ to L.
	Count 21	Count 22	Count 23	Count 24

Begin again.

Little Sister

Four wall dance. 20 counts
Music suggestion: Stetson Hat
Choreographer: Unknown

Memory jogger

Counts 1–6: Pigeon toes, dig and close R & L
Counts 7–12: Point L side, close, point R side, forward, side and hook
Counts 13–20: Vine R and hook, vine L tng L and stomp

Description with foot patterns
Counts 1–6: Pigeon toes, dig and close R & L

Pigeon toes (on the spot)	Swing heels apart.	Swing heels together.
	Count 1	Count 2

Dig and close R and L (on the spot)	Dig R heel forward.	Close R foot to L foot.	Dig L heel forward.	Close L foot to R foot without weight.
	Count 3	Count 4	Count 5	Count 6

Counts 7–12: Point L side, close, point R side, forward, side and hook

Point L side and close (on the spot)	Point L toe to side.	Close L foot to R foot.		
	Count 7	Count 8		
Point R side, forward, side and hook (on the spot)	Point R toe to side.	Point R toe forward.	Point R toe to side.	Hook R toe behind L leg.
	Count 9	Count 10	Count 11	Count 12

Counts 13–20: Vine R and hook, vine L tng L and stomp

Vine R and hook (moving R)	Step R foot to side.	Cross L foot behind R foot.	Step R foot to side.	Hook L toe behind R leg.
	Count 13	Count 14	Count 15	Count 16
Vine L tng L and stomp (moving L then tng L)	Step L foot to side.	Cross R foot behind L foot.	Step L foot to side tng 1/4 to L.	Stomp R foot next to L foot.
	Count 17	Count 18	Count 19	Count 20

Begin again.

Level 2 dance charts

Elvira Freeze

Four wall dance. 20 counts
Music suggestion: Elvira; Drinking with Both Hands
Choreographer: Unknown

Memory jogger

Counts 1–8: R & L vines
Counts 9–12: 3 walks back and kick
Counts 13–16: Step, tap, back, hitch
Counts 17–20: Forward, slide, forward tng, hitch

Description with foot patterns

Counts 1–8: R & L vines

Vine R (moving R)	Step R foot to side.	Step L foot behind R foot.	Step R foot to side.	Kick L foot across R leg, clapping hands.
	Count 1	Count 2	Count 3	Count 4
Vine L (moving L)	Step L foot to side.	Step R foot behind L foot.	Step L foot to side.	Kick R foot across L leg, clapping hands.
	Count 5	Count 6	Count 7	Count 8

Counts 9–12: 3 walks back and kick

3 walks back and kick (moving back)	Step R foot back.	Step L foot back.	Step R foot back.	Kick L foot forward, clapping hands.
	Count 9	Count 10	Count 11	Count 12

Counts 13–16: Step, tap, back, hitch

Step forward, tap, step back and hitch (on the spot)	Step L foot forward.	Tap R toe behind L foot.	Step R foot back.	Hitch L knee and clap hands.
	Count 13	Count 14	Count 15	Count 16

Counts 17–20: Forward, slide, forward tng, hitch

Step, slide, step, hitch tng ¼ L (moving forward then tng L)	Step L foot forward.	Slide R foot up to L foot.	Step L foot forward.	Hitch R knee tng ¼ to L.
	Count 17	Count 18	Count 19	Count 20

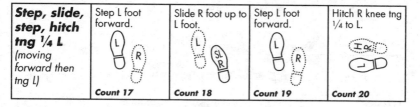

Begin again.

Note: There are other dances which also take this name but this is probably the most popular.

Catfish

Four wall dance. 32 counts
Music suggestion: The Game of Love
Choreographer: Jim Long, Jackson, Tennessee

Memory jogger

Counts 1–8: Point R twice and L twice, close
Counts 9–16: Vine L & R with scuff, ending with ¼ turn to R
Counts 17–20: 3 back steps with stomp
Counts 21–24: 2 kick, ball changes
Counts 25–32: 4 walking hip bumps

Description with foot patterns
Counts 1–8: Point R twice and L twice, close

Point close (on the spot)	Point R toe to side.	Close R foot to L foot without weight.	Point R toe to side.	Close R foot to L foot.
	Count 1	**Count 2**	**Count 3**	**Count 4**
	Point L toe to side.	Close L foot to R foot without weight.	Point L toe to side.	Touch L foot to R foot without weight.
	Count 5	**Count 6**	**Count 7**	**Count 8**

Counts 9–16: Vine L & R with scuff, ending with ¼ turn to R

L Vine (moving L)	Step L foot to side.	Cross R foot behind L foot.	Step L foot side.	Scuff R foot next to L foot.
	Count 9	**Count 10**	**Count 11**	**Count 12**
R Vine ending with turn to R (moving R and tng R)	Step R foot to side.	Cross L foot behind R foot.	Step R foot to side tng ¼ to R.	Scuff L foot next to R foot.
	Count 13	**Count 14**	**Count 15**	**Count 16**

Counts 17–20: 3 back steps with stomp

Back steps with stomp (moving back)	Step L foot back.	Step R foot back.	Step L foot back.	Stomp R foot next to L foot without weight.
	Count 17	**Count 18**	**Count 19**	**Count 20**

Counts 21–24: 2 kick, ball changes

2 kick, ball changes (on the spot)	Kick R foot forward.	Step R foot back.	Replace weight to L foot.	Kick R foot forward.
	Count 21	Count &	Count 22	Count 23
	Step R foot back.	Replace weight to L foot.		
	Count &	Count 24		

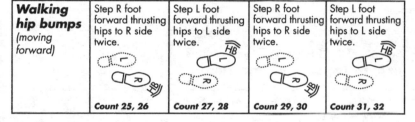

Counts 25–32: 4 walking hip bumps

Walking hip bumps (moving forward)	Step R foot forward thrusting hips to R side twice.	Step L foot forward thrusting hips to L side twice.	Step R foot forward thrusting hips to R side twice.	Step L foot forward thrusting hips to L side twice.
	Count 25, 26	Count 27, 28	Count 29, 30	Count 31, 32

Begin again.

Cowgirls' Twist

Four wall dance. 32 counts
Music suggestion: What the Cowgirls Do; Drinking with Both Hands
Choreographer: Bill Bader

Memory jogger

Counts 1–12: 4 heel struts, 3 walks back and close
Counts 13–28: Swivel heels, toes, heels, clap, twice, heels, clap, twice, heels, 3 times, clap
Counts 29–32: Step, hold, turn, hold

Description with foot patterns

Counts 1–12: 4 heel struts, 3 walks back and close

4 heel struts (moving forward)	Step R heel forward.	Drop R toe down.	Step L heel forward.	Drop L toe down.
	Count 1	Count 2	Count 3	Count 4
	Step R heel forward.	Drop R toe down.	Step L heel forward.	Drop L toe down.
	Count 5	Count 6	Count 7	Count 8
3 walks back and close (moving back)	Step R foot back.	Step L foot back.	Step L foot back.	Step L foot next to R foot.
	Count 9	Count 10	Count 11	Count 12

Counts 13–28: Swivel heels, toes, heels, clap, twice, heels, clap, twice, heels, 3 times, clap

Swivel heels, toes, heels and clap (moving L)	Swivel heels to L.	Swivel toes to L.	Swivel heels to L.	Hold position. Clap hands.
	Count 13	Count 14	Count 15	Count 16
Swivel heels,toes heels and clap (moving R)	Swivel heels to R.	Swivel toes to R.	Swivel heels to R.	Hold position. Clap hands.
	Count 17	Count 18	Count 19	Count 20
Swivel heels, clap (moving L) **Swivel heels, clap** (moving R)	Swivel heels to L.	Hold position. Clap hands.	Swivel heels to R.	Hold position. Clap hands.
	Count 21	Count 22	Count 23	Count 24

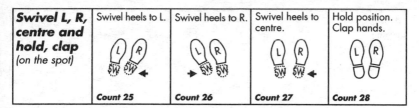

Swivel L, R, centre and hold, clap (on the spot)	Swivel heels to L.	Swivel heels to R.	Swivel heels to centre.	Hold position. Clap hands.
	Count 25	Count 26	Count 27	Count 28

Counts 29–32: Step, hold, turn, hold

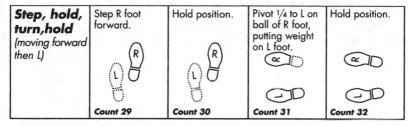

Step, hold, turn, hold (moving forward then L)	Step R foot forward.	Hold position.	Pivot ¼ to L on ball of R foot, putting weight on L foot.	Hold position.
	Count 29	Count 30	Count 31	Count 32

Begin again.

Charmaine

Four wall dance. 36 counts
Music suggestion: She's a Little Bit Country; Whisper Softly
Choreographer: Sandy Boulton

Memory jogger

Counts 1–8: Vine R & L with kicks
Counts 9–16: 3 steps back, kick, 3 steps forward, stomp
Counts 17–20: Pigeon toes
Counts 21–36: Dig, close, point back, close 3 times tng ¼ to R, kick twice, stomp twice

Description with foot patterns
Counts 1–8: Vine R & L with kicks

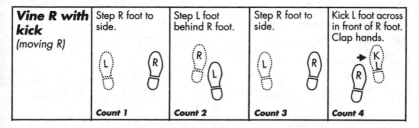

Vine R with kick (moving R)	Step R foot to side.	Step L foot behind R foot.	Step R foot to side.	Kick L foot across in front of R foot. Clap hands.
	Count 1	Count 2	Count 3	Count 4

Vine L with kick *(moving L)*	Step L foot to side.	Step R foot behind L foot.	Step L foot to side.	Kick R foot across in front of L foot. Clap hands.
	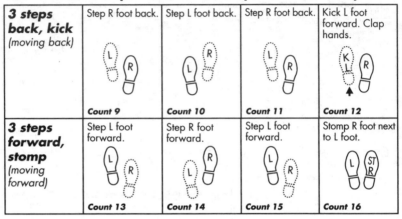			
	Count 5	Count 6	Count 7	Count 8

Counts 9–16: 3 steps back, kick, 3 steps forward, stomp

3 steps back, kick *(moving back)*	Step R foot back.	Step L foot back.	Step R foot back.	Kick L foot forward. Clap hands.
	Count 9	Count 10	Count 11	Count 12
3 steps forward, stomp *(moving forward)*	Step L foot forward.	Step R foot forward.	Step L foot forward.	Stomp R foot next to L foot.
	Count 13	Count 14	Count 15	Count 16

Counts 17–20: Pigeon toes, twice

Pigeon toes, twice *(on the spot)*	Swing heels out leaving toes together.	Swing heels back in place.	Swing heels out leaving toes together.	Swing heels back in place.
	Count 17	Count 18	Count 19	Count 20

Counts 21–36: Dig, close, point back, close 3 times tng ¼ to R, kick twice, stomp twice

Dig, close, point back *(on the spot)*	Dig R heel forward.	Close R foot to L foot.	Point L toe back.	Close L foot ro R foot.
	Count 21	Count 22	Count 23	Count 24

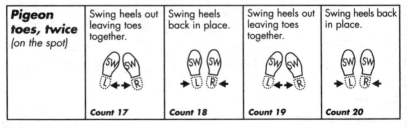
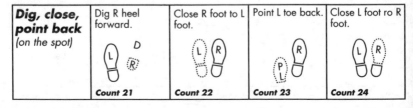

Dig, close, point back tng ⅛ to R (tng R)	Dig R heel forward tng ⅛ to R.	Close R foot to L foot.	Point L toe back.	Close L foot to R foot.
	Count 25	Count 26	Count 27	Count 28
Dig, close, point back tng ⅛ to R (tng R)	Dig R heel forward tng ⅛ to R.	Close R foot to L foot.	Point L toe back.	Close L foot to R foot.
	Count 29	Count 30	Count 31	Count 32
Kick, kick, stomp, stomp (on the spot)	Kick R foot forward twice	Stomp-up R foot next to L foot twice.		
	Count 33, 34	Count 35, 36		

Begin again.

Electric Horseman (also known as Bartender's Stomp)

Four wall dance. 24 counts
Music suggestion: Mighty Matador
Choreographer: Unknown

Memory jogger

Counts 1–12: Vine R & L with taps, 3 back steps with hitch
Counts 13–20: Forward, stomp, back hitch, forward and stomp, hold, 2 stomps
Counts 21–24: Back hitch, forward scuff and turn

Description with foot patterns
Counts 1–12: Vine R & L with taps, 3 back steps with hitch

Vine R (moving R)	Step R foot to side.	Step L foot behind R foot.	Step R foot to side.	Touch L foot next to R foot.
	Count 1	Count 2	Count 3	Count 4

Vine L (moving L)	Step L foot to side.	Step R foot behind L foot.	Step L foot to side.	Touch R foot next to L foot, clapping hands.
	Count 5	Count 6	Count 7	Count 8
3 back steps with hitch (moving back)	Back R foot.	Back L foot.	Back R foot.	Hitch L knee.
	Count 9	Count 10	Count 11	Count 12

Counts 13–20: Forward, stomp, back hitch, forward and stomps

Forward, stomp, back, hitch (forward and back)	Step L foot forward.	Stomp R foot next to L foot without weight.	Step R foot back.	Hitch L knee.
	Count 13	Count 14	Count 15	Count 16
Forward and stomps (moving forward)	Step L foot forward.	Stomp R foot next to L foot without weight.	Hold.	Stomp R foot next to L foot twice without weight.
	Count 17	Count 18	Count 19	Count & 20

Counts 21–24: Back hitch, forward scuff and turn

Back, hitch forward scuff (moving back then forward)	Step R foot back.	Hitch L leg.	Step L foot forward.	Scuff R foot tng 1/4 to L on L foot.
	Count 21	Count 22	Count 23	Count 24

Begin again.

Honky Tonk Stomp

Four wall dance. 32 counts
Music suggestion: The Sun Don't Shine on Me
Choreographer: Unknown

Memory jogger

Counts 1–16: Fans, 2 heel digs and 2 taps, heel dig and stomps R & L
Counts 17–24: Vine R and dig, vine L with hitch turn
Counts 25–32: Vine R and dig; vine L and stomp

Description with foot patterns

Counts 1–16: Fans, 2 heel digs and 2 taps, heel dig and stomps R & L

Fans *(on the spot)*	Fan R toes out. **Count 1**	Close toes together. **Count 2**	Fan R toes out. **Count 3**	Close toes together. **Count 4**
2 heel digs and 2 taps *(on the spot)*	Dig R heel forward. **Count 5**	Dig R heel forward. **Count 6**	Point R toe back. **Count 7**	Point R toe back. **Count 8**
Heel dig and stomps R & L *(on the spot)*	Dig R heel forward. **Count 9**	Stomp R foot to L foot. **Count 10**	Stomp L foot in place without weight. **Count 11**	Stomp L foot in place without weight. **Count 12**
Heel dig and stomps *(on the spot)*	Dig L heel forward. **Count 13**	Stomp L foot to R foot. **Count 14**	Stomp R foot in place without weight. **Count 15**	Stomp R foot in place without weight. **Count 16**

Counts 17–24: Vine R and dig, vine L with hitch turn

Vine R and dig (moving R)	Step R foot to side.	Cross L foot behind R foot.	Step R foot to side.	Dig L heel forward.
	Count 17	Count 18	Count 19	Count 20
Vine L, hitch turn (moving L and tng L)	Step L foot to side.	Cross R foot behind L foot.	Step L foot to side tng ½ to L.	Hitch R leg.
	Count 21	Count 22	Count 23	Count 24

Counts 25–32: Vine R and dig; vine L and stomp

Vine R and dig (moving R)	Step R foot to side.	Cross L foot behind R foot.	Step R foot to side.	Dig L heel forward.
	Count 25	Count 26	Count 27	Count 28
Vine L and stomp (moving L)	Step L foot to side.	Cross R foot behind L foot.	Step L foot to side.	Stomp R foot to L foot without weight.
	Count 29	Count 30	Count 31	Count 32

Begin again.

Level 3 dance charts

Houston Slide

Four wall dance. 22 counts
Music suggestion: Backtrack
Choreographer: Unknown

Memory jogger

Counts 1–8: Point, tap, side close to R & L
Counts 9–14: Dig twice, point twice, dig, point
Counts 15–22: Step, scuff tng, step scuff, cross, back, side, jump

Description with foot patterns

Counts 1–8: Point, tap, side close to R & L

Point, tap, side, close *(on the spot then moving R)*	Point R toe to side.	Tap R foot to L foot.	Step R foot to side.	Slide-up L foot to R foot.
	Count 1	Count 2	Count 3	Count 4
Point, close, side, close *(on the spot then moving L)*	Point L toe to side.	Tap L foot to R foot.	Step L foot to side.	Slide-up R foot to L foot.
	Count 5	Count 6	Count 7	Count 8

Counts 9–14: Dig twice, point twice, dig, point

Dig twice and point twice, then dig, point *(on the spot)*	Dig R heel forward twice.	Point R toe back twice.	Dig R heel forward.	Point R toe back.
	Count 9,10	Count 11,12	Count 13	Count 14

Counts 15–22: Step, scuff tng, step scuff, cross, back, side, jump

Step, scuff, tng, step, scuff *(moving forward, tng R then moving forward)*	Step R foot forward.	Scuff L foot next to R foot tng ¼ to R.	Step L foot forward.	Scuff R foot next to L foot.
	Count 15	Count 16	Count 17	Count 18

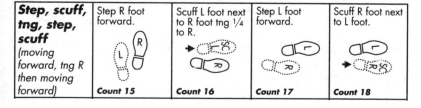

Cross, back, side, jump *(on the spot)*	Cross R foot over L foot.	Step L foot back.	Step R foot to the side.	Close L foot to R foot.
	Count 19	**Count 20**	**Count 21**	**Count 22**

Begin again.

Canadian Stomp

Four wall dance. 32 counts
Music suggestion: Hair of the Dog
Choreographer: Unknown

Memory jogger

Counts 1–16: 4 sugarfoot starting R
Counts 17–20: Back, clap twice
Counts 21–28: Side close, side, tap, twice with ¼ turn L
Counts 29–32: Jazz box

Description with foot patterns

Counts 1–16: 4 sugarfoot starting R

Sugarfoot with R foot *(moving forward)*	Point R toe into L instep.	Point R heel into L instep.	Step R foot forward.	Hold position and clap hands.
	Count 1	**Count 2**	**Count 3**	**Count 4**
Sugarfoot with L foot *(moving forward)*	Point L toe into R instep.	Point L heel into R instep.	Step L foot forward.	Hold position and clap hands.
	Count 5	**Count 6**	**Count 7**	**Count 8**

Sugarfoot with R foot (moving forward)	Point R toe into L instep.	Point R heel into L instep.	Step R foot forward.	Hold position and clap hands.
	Count 9	Count 10	Count 11	Count 12
Sugarfoot with L foot (moving forward)	Point L toe into R instep.	Point L heel into R instep.	Step L foot forward.	Hold position and clap hands.
	Count 13	Count 14	Count 15	Count 16

Counts 17–20: Back, clap twice

Back, clap twice (moving backward)	Step R foot back.	Hold position and clap hands.	Step L foot back.	Hold position and clap hands.
	Count 17	Count 18	Count 19	Count 20

Counts 21–28: Side close, side, tap, twice with ¼ turn L

Side, close, side, tap (moving R)	Step R foot to side.	Close L foot to R foot.	Step R foot to side.	Tap L foot to R foot.
	Count 21	Count 22	Count 23	Count 24
Side, close, side tng ¼ to L, tap (moving L)	Step L foot to side.	Close R foot to L foot.	Step L foot to side tng ¼ to L.	Tap R foot to L foot.
	Count 25	Count 26	Count 27	Count 28

Counts 29–32: Jazz box

Jazz box (on the spot)	Cross R foot over L foot.	Step L foot back.	Step R foot to side.	Close L foot to R foot.
	Count 29	Count 30	Count 31	Count 32

Begin again.

I Love You Too

Four wall dance. 40 counts
Music suggestion: I Love You Too
Choreographer: Ray & Tina Yeoman, UK

Memory jogger

Counts 1 - 8: Side, behind, toe strut, twice
Counts 9–16: Cross in front, hold 3 times and rock forward and back
Counts 17–24: Cross behind, hold 3 times and rock back and forward
Counts 25–36: Heel and toe struts, 3 times
Counts 37–40: Point side, tap together, forward with ¼ turn L and side

Description with foot patterns

Counts 1–8: Side, behind, toe strut, twice

Side R, behind and toe struts (moving R)	Step R foot to side.	Cross L foot behind R foot.	Step R toe to side.	Lower R heel to floor.
	Count 1	Count 2	Count 3	Count 4
Side L, behind and toe struts (moving L	Step L foot to side.	Cross R foot behind L foot.	Step L toe to the side.	Lower L heel to floor.
	Count 5	Count 6	Count 7	Count 8

Counts 9–16: Cross in front, hold 3 times and rock forward and back

Crosses in front and hold (moving forward)	Step R foot across L foot and hold position.	Step L foot across R foot and hold position.	Step R foot across L foot and hold position.
	Count 9, 10	Count 11, 12	Count 13, 14
Rock forward and back (moving forward and back)	Rock L foot forward.	Rock R foot back.	
	Count 15	Count 16	

Counts 17–24: Cross behind, hold 3 times and rock back and forward

Crosses behind and hold (moving back)	Step L foot behind R foot and hold position.	Step R foot behind L foot and hold position.	Step L foot behind R foot and hold position.
	Count 17, 18	Count 19, 20	Count 21, 22
Rocks (moving back and forward)	Rock R foot back.	Rock L foot forward.	
	Count 23	Count 24	

Counts 25–36: Heel and toe struts, three times

Heel and toe strut (moving forward then on the spot)	Step R heel forward.	Lower R toe to floor.	Step L toe next to R foot.	Lower L heel to floor.
	Count 25	Count 26	Count 27	Count 28
Heel and toe strut (moving forward then on the spot)	Step R heel forward.	Lower R toe to floor.	Step L toe next to R foot.	Lower L heel to floor.
	Count 29	Count 30	Count 31	Count 32
Heel and toe strut (moving forward then on the spot)	Step R heel forward.	Lower R toe to floor.	Step L toe next to R foot.	Lower L heel to floor.
	Count 33	Count 34	Count 35	Count 36

Counts 37–40: Point side, tap together, forward with ¼ turn L and side

Point side, tap, step turn, side (on the spot, forward then tng L)	Point R toe to side.	Tap R foot to L foot.	Step R foot forward pivoting ¼ to L.	Step L foot to side.
	Count 37	Count 38	Count 39	Count 40

Begin again.

One Step Forward

Four wall dance. 20 counts
Music suggestion: One Step Forward; Go Johnny Go
Choreographer: Betty Wilson

Memory jogger

Counts 1–10: Step forward and tap, back, close, back, tap, side, close, side, tap

Counts 11–20: Step forward, tap, back, close, back, tap, side, close, side, hitch with turn

Description with foot patterns

Counts 1–10: Step forward and tap, back, close, back, tap, side, close, side, tap

Step forward, and tap (moving forward)	Step L foot diagonally forward. Count 1	Touch R foot behind L foot without weight. Count 2		
Step back, close, back and tap (moving back)	Step R foot diagonally back. Count 3	Step L foot next to R foot. Count 4	Step R foot diagonally back. Count 5	Touch L foot next to R foot without weight. Count 6
Side, close, side, tap (moving L)	Step L foot to side. Count 7	Close R foot next to L foot. Count 8	Step L foot to side. Count 9	Touch R foot next to L foot without weight. Count 10

Counts 11–20: Step forward, tap, back, close, back, tap, side, close, side, hitch with turn

Step forward, and tap (moving forward)	Step R foot diagonally forward.	Touch L foot behind R foot without weight.		
	Count 11	Count 12		
Step back, close, back and tap (moving back)	Step L foot diagonally back.	Step R foot next to L foot.	Step L foot diagonally back.	Touch R foot next to L foot without weight.
	Count 13	Count 14	Count 15	Count 16
Side, close, side, hitch (moving R then tng R)	Step R foot to side.	Step L foot next to R foot.	Step R foot to side.	Hitch L knee tng 1/4 to R on ball of R foot.
	Count 17	Count 18	Count 19	Count 20

Begin again.

Variation 1

In some regions, the forward and backward steps are taken directly forward and back rather than on the diagonal.

Variation 2

On the forward and backward steps a sliding action may be used.

Reggae Cowboy

Four wall dance. 32 counts
Music suggestion: Reggae Cowboy
Choreographer: Montana

Memory jogger

Counts 1–8: Point R, forward, point L, forward. Repeat

Counts 9–16: Cross R toe in front of L leg, kick, shuffle, repeat L

Counts 17–24: 4 walks tng R, 4 walks tng L

Counts 25–32: 3 walks forward and kick, 3 walks back with turn L and stomp

Description with foot patterns

Counts 1–8: Point R, forward, point L, forward. Repeat

Point R forward, point L forward (moving forward)	Point R foot to side.	Step R foot forward.	Point L foot to side.	Step L foot forward.
	Count 1	Count 2	Count 3	Count 4
	Point R foot to side.	Step R foot forward.	Point L foot to side.	Step L foot forward.
	Count 5	Count 6	Count 7	Count 8

Counts 9–16: Cross R toe in front of L leg, kick, shuffle, repeat L

Cross R toe in front of L leg, kick (on the spot)	Cross R toe in front of L leg.	Kick R foot forward.	
	Count 9	Count 10	
Shuffle back (moving back)	Step R foot back.	Step L foot toward R foot.	Step R foot back.
	Count 11	Count &	Count 12

| **Cross L toe in front of R leg, kick** (on the spot) | Cross L toe in front of R leg.

 Count 13 | Kick L foot forward.

 Count 14 | |
| **Shuffle back** (moving back) | Step L foot back.

 Count 15 | Step R foot toward L foot.

 Count & | Step L foot back.

 Count 16 |

Counts 17–24: 4 walks tng R, 4 walks tng L

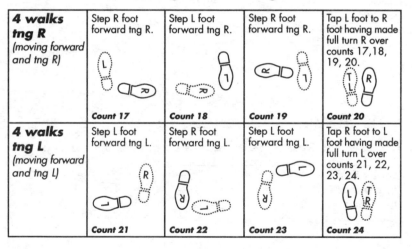

| **4 walks tng R** (moving forward and tng R) | Step R foot forward tng R.

 Count 17 | Step L foot forward tng R.

 Count 18 | Step R foot forward tng R.

 Count 19 | Tap L foot to R foot having made full turn R over counts 17,18, 19, 20.

 Count 20 |
| **4 walks tng L** (moving forward and tng L) | Step L foot forward tng L.

 Count 21 | Step R foot forward tng L.

 Count 22 | Step L foot forward tng L.

 Count 23 | Tap R foot to L foot having made full turn L over counts 21, 22, 23, 24.

 Count 24 |

Counts 25–32: 3 walks forward and kick, 3 walks back with turn L and stomp

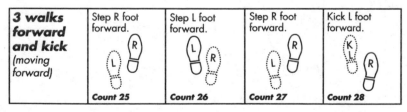

| **3 walks forward and kick** (moving forward) | Step R foot forward.

 Count 25 | Step L foot forward.

 Count 26 | Step R foot forward.

 Count 27 | Kick L foot forward.

 Count 28 |

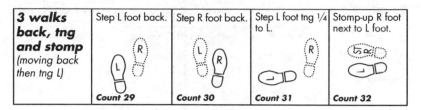

3 walks back, tng and stomp (moving back then tng L)	Step L foot back. Count 29	Step R foot back. Count 30	Step L foot tng ¼ to L. Count 31	Stomp-up R foot next to L foot. Count 32

Begin again.

Hardwood Stomp

Four wall dance. 32 counts
Music suggestion: Heartbeat or Hardwood Stomp
Choreographer: Unknown

Memory jogger

Counts 1–8: Side L, close, side L, tap, side R, tap, side L, tap
Counts 9–16: Side R, close, side R, tap, side L, tap, side R, tap
Counts 17–24: Forward L, slide, forward, slide, back R, slide for 2 beats, clap
Counts 25–32: Dig R, clap, tap R back, clap, forward R, turn ¼ L, side stomp R, clap

Description with foot patterns

Counts 1–8: Side L, close, side L, tap, side R, tap, side L, tap

Side L, close, side, tap (moving L)	Step L foot to side. Count 1	Close R foot to L foot. Count 2	Step L foot to side. Count 3	Tap R foot next to L foot. Count 4
Side R, tap, side L, tap (moving R then L)	Step R foot to side. Count 5	Tap L foot next to R foot. Count 6	Step L foot to side. Count 7	Tap R foot next to L foot. Count 8

Counts 9–16: Side R, close, side R, tap, side L, tap, side R, tap

Side R, close, side R, tap (moving R)	Step R foot to side.	Close L foot to R foot.	Step R foot to side.	Tap L foot next to R foot.
	Count 9	Count 10	Count 11	Count 12
Side L, tap, side R, tap (moving L then R)	Step L foot to side.	Tap R foot next to L foot.	Step R foot to side.	Tap L foot next to R foot.
	Count 13	Count 14	Count 15	Count 16

Counts 17–24: Forward L, slide, forward, slide, back R, slide for 2 beats, clap

Forward, slide, twice (moving forward)	Step L foot forward.	Slide R foot behind L foot.	Step L foot forward.	Slide-up R foot behind L foot.
	Count 17	Count 18	Count 19	Count 20
Back slide for 2 beats, clap (moving back then on the spot)	Step R foot back.	Slide L foot to R foot. Take two counts.	Hold position and clap hands.	
	Count 21	Count 22, 23	Count 24	

Counts 25–32: Dig R, clap, tap R back, clap, forward R, turn ¼ L, side stomp R, clap

Dig R, clap, tap back, clap (on the spot)	Dig R heel forward.	Hold position and clap hands.	Tap R toe back.	Hold position and clap hands.
	Count 25	Count 26	Count 27	Count 28

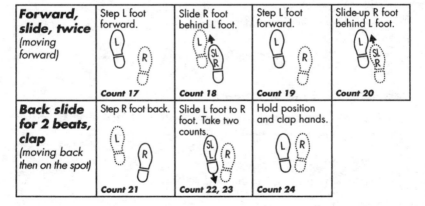

Forward R turn ¼ L, stomp and clap (forward, turn L, then on the spot)	Step R foot forward tng ¼ to L.	Step L foot to side.	Stomp R foot next to L foot.	Hold position and clap hands.
	Count 29	**Count 30**	**Count 31**	**Count 32**

Begin again.

Note: There are several other versions of this dance.

Level 4 dance charts

Cowboy Motion

Four wall dance. 24 counts
Music suggestion: Me and My Baby
Choreographer: Unknown

Memory jogger

Counts 1–12: Vine R, L then 3 steps back and stomp
Counts 13–24: 2 toe taps, 2 heel digs, toe tap, heel dig, switch, clap and hip bumps

Description with foot patterns
Counts 1–12: Vine R, L then 3 steps back and stomp

Vine R (moving R)	Step R foot to side.	Step L foot behind R foot.	Step R foot to side.	Tap L foot to R foot.
	Count 1	**Count 2**	**Count 3**	**Count 4**
Vine L (moving L)	Step L foot to side.	Step R foot behind L foot.	Step L foot to side.	Tap R foot to L foot.
	Count 5	**Count 6**	**Count 7**	**Count 8**

3 steps back and stomp (moving backwards)	Step R foot back.	Step L foot back.	Step R foot back.	Stomp L foot to R foot without weight.
	Count 9	Count 10	Count 11	Count 12

Counts 13–24: 2 toe taps, 2 heel digs, toe tap, heel dig, switch, clap and hip bumps

2 toe tap and 2 heel digs (on the spot)	Tap L toe to side.	Tap L toe to side.	Dig L heel forward across R leg.	Dig L heel forward across R leg.
	Count 13	Count 14	Count 15	Count 16
Toe tap and heel dig (on the spot)	Tap L toe to side.	Dig L heel forward across R leg.		
	Count 17	Count 18		
Switch (on the spot)	Close L foot to R foot.	Dig R heel forward.	Hold position and clap hands.	
	Count &	Count 19	Count 20	
Hip bumps (tng L)	Tng ¼ to L bump hips twice to R.	Bump hips twice to L.		
	Count 21, 22	Count 23, 24		

Begin again.

Flying Eight (sometimes known as Flying Eights)

Two wall dance. 20 counts
Music suggestion: Dancing Feet
Choreographer: Unknown

Memory jogger

Counts 1–4: Vine L with R hitch
Counts 5–8: Vine R with ¼ turn R with L hitch
Counts 9–12: Vine L with ¾ turn L with R hitch
Counts 13–24: Forward R, L, R with L hitch, step hitch R, step hitch L

Description with foot patterns
Counts 1–4: Vine L with R hitch

Vine L with R hitch (moving L)	Step L foot to side.	Cross R foot behind L foot.	Step L foot to side.	Hitch R leg.
	Count 1	Count 2	Count 3	Count 4

Counts 5–8: Vine R with ¼ turn R with L hitch

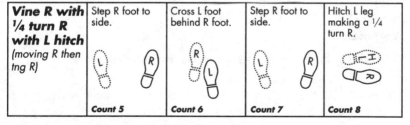

Vine R with ¼ turn R with L hitch (moving R then tng R)	Step R foot to side.	Cross L foot behind R foot.	Step R foot to side.	Hitch L leg making a ¼ turn R.
	Count 5	Count 6	Count 7	Count 8

Counts 9–12: Vine L with ¾ turn L & R hitch

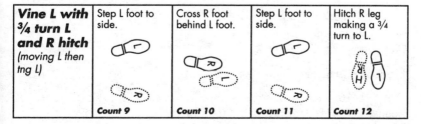

Vine L with ¾ turn L and R hitch (moving L then tng L)	Step L foot to side.	Cross R foot behind L foot.	Step L foot to side.	Hitch R leg making a ¾ turn to L.
	Count 9	Count 10	Count 11	Count 12

Counts 13–20: Forward R, L, R with L hitch, step hitch R, step hitch L

Forward R, L, R with L hitch *(moving forward)*	Step R foot forward.	Step L foot forward.	Step R foot forward.	Hitch L leg.
	Count 13	Count 14	Count 15	Count 16
Step hitch R, step hitch L *(moving forward)*	Step L foot forward.	Hitch R leg.	Step R foot forward.	Hitch L leg.
	Count 17	Count 18	Count 19	Count 20

Begin again.

Note: There are one or two different variations to this dance.

Variation 1

In some regions it is danced as below:

Counts 1–5: Three kicks L, R, L
Counts 6–17: Vine L, Vine R with ¼ turn R, Vine L with ¾ turn L
Counts 18–20: Three stomps R, L, R

Variation 2

In other regions it only has 18 counts and is danced as below:

Counts 1–12: As in foot chart above.
Counts 13–18: Step R foot, hitch L leg, step L foot, hitch R leg, step R foot, hitch L leg

Cross My Heart

Two wall dance. 32 counts
Music suggestion: I Don't Know
Choreographer: Gita Renick

Memory jogger

Counts 1–16: Kick, ball, cross, shuffle, rocks and pivot R & L
Counts 17–24: Diagonal forward toe struts R, L, R, L
Counts 25–32: 2 jazz boxes with ¼ turns R

Description with foot patterns
Counts 1–16: Kick, ball, cross, shuffle, rocks and pivot R & L

R kick, ball, cross (on the spot)	Kick R foot forward. Count 1	Step R foot back. Count &	Cross L foot over R foot. Count 2	
Shuffle (moving R)	Step R foot to side. Count 3	Step L foot towards R foot. Count &	Step R foot to side. Count 4	
Rock, rock and pivot 1/2 turn R (on the spot then tng to R)	Rock L foot back. Count 5	Rock R foot in place. Count 6	Step L foot forward pivoting 1/2 turn to R. Count 7	Replace weight to R foot. Count 8
L kick, ball, cross (on the spot)	Kick L foot forward. Count 9	Step L foot back. Count &	Cross R foot over L foot. Count 10	
Shuffle (moving L)	Step L foot to side. Count 11	Step R foot towards L foot. Count &	Step L foot to side. Count 12	
Rock, rock and pivot 1/2 turn L (on the spot then tng to L)	Rock R foot back. Count 13	Rock L foot in place. Count 14	Step R foot forward pivoting 1/2 turn to L. Count 15	Replace weight to L foot. Count 16

Counts 17–24: Diagonal forward toe struts R, L, R, L

Diagonal forward toe struts R, L *(moving diagonally forward to L)*	Step R toe diagonally forward across L foot. Count 17	Slap R heel to floor. Count 18	Step L toe to side. Count 19	Slap L heel to floor. Count 20
Diagonal forward toe struts R, L *(moving diagonally forward to L)*	Step R toe diagonally forward across L foot. Count 21	Slap R heel to floor. Count 22	Step L toe to side. Count 23	Slap L heel to floor. Count 24

Counts 25–32: 2 jazz boxes with ¼ turns R

Jazz box with ¼ turn to R *(on the spot then tng R)*	Cross R foot over L foot. Count 25	Step L foot back. Count 26	Step R foot to side making ¼ turn to R. Count 27	Close L foot to R foot. Count 28
Jazz box with ¼ turn to R *(on the spot then tng R)*	Cross R foot over L foot. Count 29	Step L foot back. Count 30	Step R foot to side making ¼ turn to R. Count 31	Close L foot to R foot. Count 32

Begin again.

Texas Stomp

Two wall dance. 32 counts
Music suggestion: Down on the Farm
Choreographer: Ruth Elias, GB

Memory jogger

Counts 1–8: 3 steps forward and kick, 3 steps back and stomp
Counts 9–16: Side, close, side, stomp R & L
Counts 17–24: Side, stomp R & L, forward, stomp and back, stomp
Counts 25–32: Forward, slide, forward, scuff, forward, slide, forward, turn L

Description with foot patterns

Counts 1–8: 3 steps forward and kick, 3 steps back and stomp

3 steps forward and kick *(moving forward)*	Step R foot forward.	Step L foot forward.	Step R foot forward.	Kick L foot forward.
	Count 1	**Count 2**	**Count 3**	**Count 4**
3 steps back and stomp *(moving back)*	Step L foot back.	Step R foot back.	Step L foot back.	Stomp R foot next to L foot without weight.
	Count 5	**Count 6**	**Count 7**	**Count 8**

Counts 9–16: Side, close, side, stomp R & L

Side, close, side, stomp *(moving R)*	Step R foot to side.	Close L foot to R foot.	Step R foot to side.	Stomp L foot next to R foot without weight.
	Count 9	**Count 10**	**Count 11**	**Count 12**
Side, close, side, stomp *(moving L)*	Step L foot to side.	Close R foot next to L foot.	Step L foot to side.	Stomp R foot next to L foot without weight.
	Count 13	**Count 14**	**Count 15**	**Count 16**

Counts 17–24: Side, stomp R & L, forward, stomp and back, stomp

Side and stomp R & L (moving R then L)	Step R foot to side.	Stomp-up L foot next to R foot.	Step L foot to side.	Stomp R foot next to L foot without weight.
	Count 17	Count 18	Count 19	Count 20
Forward, stomp and back stomp (moving forward and back)	Step R foot forward.	Stomp-up L foot next to R foot.	Step L foot back.	Stomp R foot next to L foot without weight.
	Count 21	Count 22	Count 23	Count 24

Counts 25–32: Forward, slide, forward scuff, forward, slide, forward, turn

Forward, slide, forward, scuff (moving forward)	Step R foot forward.	Slide L foot up to R foot.	Step R foot forward.	Scuff L foot next to R foot.
	Count 25	Count 26	Count 27	Count 28
Forward, slide, forward, turn L (moving forward then tng L)	Step L foot forward.	Slide R foot next to L foot.	Step L foot forward.	Pivot 1/2 turn L on ball of L foot.
	Count 29	Count 30	Count 31	Count 32

Begin again.

Cowboy Strut

Two wall dance. 32 counts
Music Suggestion: And I Worry
Choreographer: Unknown

Memory jogger

Counts 1–8: Heel fans R, L, R, L
Counts 9–16: 2 heel digs, 2 toe points, 1 heel dig, clap, 1 toe point, clap
Counts 17–24: 4 heel struts
Counts 25–32: 2 jazz boxes, tng

Description with foot patterns
Counts 1–8: Heel fans R, L, R, L

Heel fans R, L, R, L *(on the spot)*	Fan R heel out to side while toes remain together.	Close heels together.	Fan L heel out to side while toes remain together.	Close heels together.
	Count 1	**Count 2**	**Count 3**	**Count 4**
	Fan R heel out to side while toes remain together.	Close heels together.	Fan L heel out to side while toes remain together.	Close heels together.
	Count 5	**Count 6**	**Count 7**	**Count 8**

Counts 9–16: 2 heel digs, 2 toe points, 1 heel dig, clap, 1 toe point, clap

2 digs and 2 toe points, dig, clap, point clap *(on the spot)*	Dig R heel forward twice.	Point R toe back twice.	Dig R heel forward.	Hold position and clap hands.
	Count 9, 10	**Count 11, 12**	**Count 13**	**Count 14**

Point R toe back.	Hold position and clap hands.
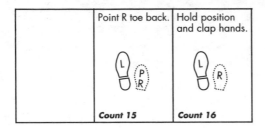	
Count 15	**Count 16**

Counts 17–24: 4 heel struts

4 heel struts (moving forward)	Step R heel forward.	Lower R toe to the floor.	Step L heel forward.	Lower L toe to the floor.
	Count 17	**Count 18**	**Count 19**	**Count 20**
	Step R heel forward.	Lower R toe to the floor.	Step L heel forward.	Lower L toe to the floor.
	Count 21	**Count 22**	**Count 23**	**Count 24**

Counts 25–32: 2 jazz boxes, tng

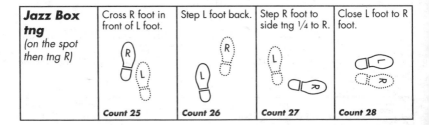

Jazz Box tng (on the spot then tng R)	Cross R foot in front of L foot.	Step L foot back.	Step R foot to side tng ¼ to R.	Close L foot to R foot.
	Count 25	**Count 26**	**Count 27**	**Count 28**

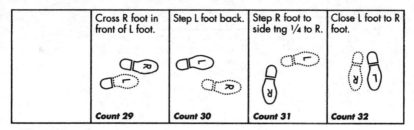

Cross R foot in front of L foot.	Step L foot back.	Step R foot to side tng ¼ to R.	Close L foot to R foot.
Count 29	**Count 30**	**Count 31**	**Count 32**

Begin again.

State Line Waltz

4 wall dance. 24 counts

Music suggestion: (Who Says) You Can't Have It All; More Than One Heart

Choreographer: Dave & Di Doyle

Memory jogger

Counts 1–6: L twinkle and R twinkle
Counts 7–12: ½ turn L & rock steps
Counts 13–18: Repeat counts 7–12
Counts 19–24: ¼ L and basic twinkle back

Description with foot patterns
Counts 1–6: L twinkle and R twinkle

L twinkle *(on the spot)*	Cross L foot over R foot.	Step R foot to the R side.	Step L foot in place.
	Count 1	**Count 2**	**Count 3**
R twinkle *(on the spot)*	Cross R foot over L foot.	Step L foot to the L side.	Step R foot in place.
	Count 4	**Count 5**	**Count 6**

Counts 7–12: ½ turn L & rock steps

½ *turn L* (forward then tng L)	Step L foot forward.	Swivel ½ to L on ball of L foot. Step R foot next to L foot.	Step L foot in place.
	Count 7	Count 8	Count 9
Rock steps (on the spot)	Step R foot to side.	Rock weight to L foot.	Rock weight to R foot.
	Count 10	Count 11	Count 12

Counts 13–18: Repeat counts 7–12
Counts 19–24: ¼ L and basic twinkle back

¼ *turn L* (forward then tng L)	Step L foot forward.	Swivel ¼ turn to L on ball of L foot. Step R foot next to L foot.	Step L foot in place.
	Count 19	Count 20	Count 21
Twinkle back (moving back)	Step R foot back.	Step L foot beside R foot.	Step R foot in place.
	Count 22	Count 23	Count 24

Begin again.

Level 5 dance charts

Texan Boogie

Four wall dance. 46 counts
Music suggestion: A1 Blues
Choreographer: Texan Tempros

Memory jogger

Counts 1–16: Heel fans R & L and digs R & L. Repeat
Counts 17–32: 2 Charlestons
Counts 33–36: Pivot turn, stomp, stomp
Counts 37–44: Struts and hitches

Description with foot patterns
Counts 1–16: Heel fans R & L and digs R & L. Repeat

Heel fans *individually* (on the spot)	Fan R heel to R.	Close R heel to L heel.	Fan L heel to L.	Close L heel to R heel.
	Count 1	**Count 2**	**Count 3**	**Count 4**
Dig R heel *and L heel* (on the spot)	Dig R heel forward.	Close R foot to L foot.	Dig L heel forward.	Close L foot to R foot.
	Count 5	**Count 6**	**Count 7**	**Count 8**
Heel fans *individually* (on the spot)	Fan R heel to R.	Close R heel to L heel.	Fan L heel to L.	Close L heel to R heel.
	Count 9	**Count 10**	**Count 11**	**Count 12**
Dig R heel *and L heel* (on the spot)	Dig R heel forward.	Close R foot to L foot.	Dig L heel forward.	Close L foot to R foot.
	Count 13	**Count 14**	**Count 15**	**Count 16**

Counts 17–32: 2 Charlestons

Charleston (moving forward then back)	Step R foot forward taking two counts.	Tap L foot forward taking two counts.	Step L foot back taking two counts.	Tap R foot back taking two counts.
	Count 17, 18	*Count 19, 20*	*Count 21, 22*	*Count 23, 24*
	Step R foot forward taking two counts.	Tap L foot forward taking two counts.	Step L foot back taking two counts.	Tap R foot back taking two counts.
	Count 25, 26	*Count 27, 28*	*Count 29, 30*	*Count 31, 32*

Counts 33–36: Pivot turn, stomp, stomp

Pivot turn, stomp, stomp (tng L then on the spot)	Step R foot forward and tng ¼ L.	Replace weight to L foot.	Stomp R foot in place.	Stomp L foot in place.
	Count 33	*Count 34*	*Count 35*	*Count 36*

Counts 37–44: Struts and hitches

Struts (moving forward)	Step R heel forward.	Lower R toes to floor.	Step L heel forward.	Lower L toes to floor.
	Count 37	*Count 38*	*Count 39*	*Count 40*

Hitches *(on the spot)*	Hitch R leg in front of L leg touching heel with L hand.	Stomp R foot in place without weight.	Hitch R leg out to R side touching heel with R hand.	Stomp-up R foot in place.
	Count 41	**Count 42**	**Count 43**	**Count 44**

Begin again.

Bus Stop

Four wall dance. 16 counts
Music suggestion: Dancing Feet
Choreographer: Unknown

Memory jogger

Counts 1–8: Side R, close, side, tap, side L, close, side, tap
Counts 9–12: Heel dig R, toe point R, forward tng ¼ R, tap
Counts 13–16: Cross L, tap, cross R, step back L

Description with foot patterns
Counts 1–8: Side R, close, side, tap, side L, close, side, tap

Side R, *close, side,* *tap* *(moving R)*	Step R foot to side.	Close L foot to R foot.	Step R foot to side.	Tap L foot next to R foot.
	Count 1	**Count 2**	**Count 3**	**Count 4**
Side L, *close, side,* *tap* *(moving L)*	Step L foot to side.	Close R foot to L foot.	Step L foot to side.	Tap R foot next to L foot.
	Count 5	**Count 6**	**Count 7**	**Count 8**

Counts 9–12: Heel dig R, toe point R, forward tng ¼ R, tap

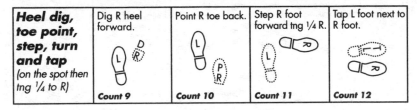

Heel dig, toe point, step, turn and tap (on the spot then tng ¼ to R)	Dig R heel forward.	Point R toe back.	Step R foot forward tng ¼ R.	Tap L foot next to R foot.
	Count 9	Count 10	Count 11	Count 12

Counts 13–16: Cross L, tap, cross R, step back L

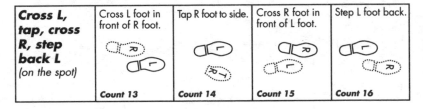

Cross L, tap, cross R, step back L (on the spot)	Cross L foot in front of R foot.	Tap R foot to side.	Cross R foot in front of L foot.	Step L foot back.
	Count 13	Count 14	Count 15	Count 16

Begin again.

Note: Watch out. You will find there are other completely different dances using the same name as this.

Ski Bumpus (also known as Black Velvet or White Horse)

One wall dance. 40 counts
Music suggestion: Modification
Choreographer: Linda DeFord

Memory jogger

Counts 1–12: 2 shuffles and a pivot twice
Counts 13–20: 2 jazz boxes
Counts 21–28: Four 'point and walks'
Counts 29–40: 2 kick, ball changes and a pivot twice

Description with foot patterns
Counts 1–12: 2 shuffles and a pivot twice

Shuffles and a pivot (moving forward then tng L)	Step R foot forward.	L foot closes up towards R foot.	Step R foot forward.	Step L foot forward.
	Count 1	Count &	Count 2	Count 3
	R foot closes up towards L foot.	Step L foot forward.	Step R foot forward then pivot ½ L to face opposite wall.	Step L foot forward.
	Count &	Count 4	Count 5	Count 6

Counts 7–12: As for counts 1–6

Counts 13–20: 2 jazz boxes

2 Jazz boxes (on the spot)	Step R foot across in front of L foot.	Step L foot back.	Step R foot to R side.	Close L foot to R foot.
	Count 13	Count 14	Count 15	Count 16
	Step R foot across in front of L foot.	Step L foot back.	Step R foot to R side.	Close L foot to R foot.
	Count 17	Count 18	Count 19	Count 20

Counts 21–28: Four 'point and walks'

Four 'point and walks' (moving forward)	Point R foot to side.	Step R foot forward.	Point L foot to side.	Step L foot forward.
	Count 21	Count 22	Count 23	Count 24

Point R foot to side.	Step R foot forward.	Point L foot to side.	Step L foot forward.
Count 25	Count 26	Count 27	Count 28

Counts 29–40: 2 kick, ball changes and a pivot twice

Kick, ball changes and pivot *(on the spot then tng L)*	Kick R foot forward.	Step R foot back on ball of foot.	Transfer weight to ball of L foot.	Kick R foot forward.
	Count 29	Count &	Count 30	Count 31
	Step R foot back on ball of foot.	Transfer weight to ball of L foot.	Step R foot forward then pivot ½ L to face opposite wall.	Step L foot forward.
	Count &	Count 32	Count 33	Count 34
Kick, ball changes and pivot *(on the spot then tng L)*	Kick R foot forward.	Step R foot back on ball of foot.	Transfer weight to ball of L foot.	Kick R foot forward.
	Count 35	Count &	Count 36	Count 37
	Step R foot back on ball of foot.	Transfer weight to ball of L foot.	Step R foot forward then pivot ½ L to face opposite wall.	Step L foot forward.
	Count &	Count 38	Count 39	Count 40

Begin again.

Note: There are two regional variations to this dance.

Variation 1

The pivot turns on Counts 39 & 40 may be danced ¼ turn to L instead of ½ turn. This will make it a four wall dance.

Variation 2

The 'point and walk' on Counts 21–28 can be danced point and then close rather than point and then forward. This will mean Counts 21–28 are danced on the spot rather than moving forward.

Ski Bumpus (Black Velvet/White Horse) may also be danced in lines facing each other.

Cowboy ChaCha

Four wall dance. 20 counts
Music suggestion: Because You're Mine; Wish you Were Here
Choreographer: Unknown

Memory jogger

Counts 1–4: Step forward L, replace and shuffle back
Counts 5–16: Step back, replace, shuffle tng, 3 times
Counts 17–20: 2 pivots

Description with foot patterns

Counts 1–4: Step forward L, replace and shuffle back

Step forward L, replace (on the spot)	Step L foot forward.	Replace weight back to R foot.	
	Count 1	Count 2	
Shuffle (moving back)	Step L foot back.	Step R foot towards L foot.	Step L foot back.
	Count 3	Count &	Count 4

Counts 5–16: Step back, replace, shuffle tng, 3 times

R foot back, replace (on the spot)	Step R foot back. **Count 5**	Replace weight forward to L foot. **Count 6**	
Shuffle tng (tng L)	Step R foot forward tng L. **Count 7**	Step L foot towards R foot still tng L. **Count &**	Step R foot forward tng L. ½ turn over counts 7 & 8. **Count 8**
L foot back and replace (on the spot)	Step L foot back. **Count 9**	Replace weight forward to R foot. **Count 10**	
Shuffle (tng R)	Step L foot forward tng R. **Count 11**	Step R foot towards L foot still tng R. **Count &**	Step L foot forward tng R. ½ turn over counts 11 & 12. **Count 12**
R foot back, replace (on the spot)	Step R foot back. **Count 13**	Replace weight forward to L foot. **Count 14**	
Shuffle (tng L)	Step R foot forward tng L. **Count 15**	Step L foot towards R foot still tng L. **Count &**	Step R foot forward tng L. ¼ turn over counts 15 & 16. **Count 16**

Counts 17–20: Pivots

2 pivot turns (tng R)	Step L foot forward pivoting ½ turn to R.	Step R foot forward.	Step L foot forward pivoting ½ turn to R.	Step R foot forward.
	Count 17	Count 18	Count 19	Count 20

Begin again.

Note: A different variation to this dance is for Counts 17–20 to be danced without turn.

The Bubba

Four wall dance. 34 counts
Music suggestion: Cleopatra; Best of Friends
Choreographer: Unknown

Memory jogger

Counts 1–6: Dig R, close, swivels
Counts 7–16: Dig R, hook R and swivels
Counts 17–20: Hook L
Counts 21–28: Step L, tap R and back twice
Counts 29–34: Step L, stomp tng ¼ L, back, back, stomp, stomp

Description with foot patterns

Counts 1–6: Dig R, close, swivels

Dig R and close (on the spot)	Dig R heel forward.	Close R foot to L foot.		
	Count 1	Count 2		
Swivels (on the spot)	Swivel heels to R.	Swivel heels to L.	Swivel heels to R.	Swivel heels to centre.
	Count 3	Count 4	Count 5	Count 6

Counts 7–16: Dig R, hook R and swivels

Dig R and close (on the spot)	Dig R heel forward.	Close R foot to L foot.		
	  Count 7	 Count 8		
Hook R (on the spot)	Dig R heel forward.	Hook R heel in front of L knee.	Dig R heel forward.	Close R foot to L foot.
	  Count 9	 Count 10	 Count 11	 Count 12
Swivels (on the spot)	Swivel heels to R.	Swivel heels to L.	Swivel heels to R.	Swivel heels to centre.
	  Count 13	 Count 14	 Count 15	 Count 16

Counts 17–20: Hook L

Hook L (on the spot)	Dig L heel forward.	Hook L heel in front of R knee.	Dig L heel forward.	Close L foot to R foot without weight.
	  Count 17	 Count 18	 Count 19	 Count 20

Counts 21–28: Step L, tap R and back twice

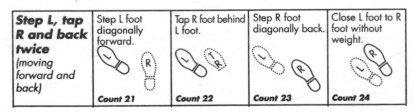

Step L, tap R and back twice (moving forward and back)	Step L foot diagonally forward.	Tap R foot behind L foot.	Step R foot diagonally back.	Close L foot to R foot without weight.
	  Count 21	 Count 22	 Count 23	 Count 24

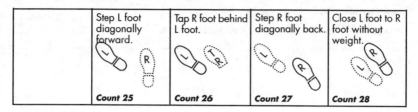

	Step L foot diagonally forward.	Tap R foot behind L foot.	Step R foot diagonally back.	Close L foot to R foot without weight.
	Count 25	**Count 26**	**Count 27**	**Count 28**

Counts 29–34: Step L, stomp tng ¼ L, back, back, stomp, stomp

Step L, stomp tng ¼ L (moving forward then tng ¼ L)	Step L foot diagonally forward.	Stomp R foot to L foot tng ¼ to L without weight.		
	Count 29	**Count 30**		
Back twice, stomp twice (moving back then on the spot)	Step back R foot.	Step back L foot.	Stomp R foot next to L foot without weight.	Stomp R foot next to L foot without weight.
	Count 31	**Count 32**	**Count 33**	**Count 34**

Begin again.

Chattahoochee

Four wall dance. 28 counts
Music suggestion: Chattahoochee; All Dressed Up
Choreographer: Unknown

Memory jogger

Counts 1–16: Hooks and swivels L & R
Counts 17–28: Side slap R & L, side tng, slide, forward, clap, 3 walks back and stomp

Description with foot patterns
Counts 1–16: Hooks and swivels L & R

Hook L *(on the spot)*	Dig L heel diagonally forward. **Count 1**	Hook L foot in front of R leg. **Count 2**	Dig L heel diagonally forward. **Count 3**	Step L foot next to R foot. **Count 4**
Swivels L *(on the spot)*	Swivel heels to L. **Count 5**	Swivel heels to centre. **Count 6**	Swivel heels to L. **Count 7**	Swivel heels to centre. **Count 8**
Hook R *(on the spot)*	Dig R heel diagonally forward. **Count 9**	Hook R foot in front of L leg. **Count 10**	Dig R heel diagonally forward. **Count 11**	Step R foot next to L foot. **Count 12**
Swivels R *(on the spot)*	Swivel heels to R. **Count 13**	Swivel heels to centre. **Count 14**	Swivel heels to R. **Count 15**	Swivel heels to centre. **Count 16**

Counts 17–28: Side slap R & L, side tng, slide, forward, clap, 3 walks back and stomp

Side slaps R & L *(on the spot)*	Step R foot to R side. **Count 17**	Hook L leg behind R leg and slap L heel with R hand. **Count 18**	Step L foot to L side. **Count 19**	Hook R leg behind L leg and slap R heel with L hand. **Count 20**

Side tng, slide, forward, tap (moving to R tng 1/4 then forward)	Step R foot to side tng 1/4 to R.	Slide L foot to R foot.	Step R foot forward.	Touch L foot to R foot and clap hands.
	Count 21	**Count 22**	**Count 23**	**Count 24**
3 walks back and stomp (moving back)	Step L foot back.	Step R foot back.	Step L foot back.	Stomp R foot next to L foot.
	Count 25	**Count 26**	**Count 27**	**Count 28**

Begin again.

Level 6 dance charts

Cheyenne

Four wall dance. 24 counts
Music suggestion: A1 Blues
Choreographer: Unknown

Memory jogger

Counts 1–8: 2 digs L, 2 digs R with hitch turn to L
Counts 9–16: 3 walks back, forward, slide, forward, tap
Counts 17–24: Cross in front, side, cross behind, tap. Repeat ending in close

Description with foot patterns

Counts 1–8: 2 digs L, 2 digs R with hitch turn to L

2 digs L (on the spot)	Dig L heel forward.	Close L foot ro R foot without weight.	Dig L heel forward.	Close L foot to R foot.
	Count 1	**Count 2**	**Count 3**	**Count 4**

2 digs R, *with hitch* *turn to L* (on the spot then tng L)	Dig R heel forward.	Close R foot to L foot without weight.	Dig R heel forward.	Hitch R leg tng ¼ to L.
	Count 5	Count 6	Count 7	Count 8

Counts 9–16: 3 walks back, forward, slide, forward, tap

3 walks *back with a* *tap* (moving back)	Step R foot back.	Step L foot back.	Step R foot back.	Tap L foot next to R foot.
	Count 9	Count 10	Count 11	Count 12
Forward, *slide,* *forward,* *tap* (omoving forward)	Step L foot forward.	Slide R foot to L foot.	Step L foot forward.	Tap R foot next to L foot.
	Count 13	Count 14	Count 15	Count 16

Counts 17–24: Cross in front, side, cross behind, tap. Repeat ending in close

Cross, side, *cross touch* (moving L)	Cross R foot in front of L foot.	Step L foot to side.	Cross R foot behind L foot.	Tap L foot to side.
	Count 17	Count 18	Count 19	Count 20
Cross, side, *cross close* (moving R)	Cross L foot in front of R foot.	Step R foot to side.	Cross L foot behind R foot.	Close R foot to L foot.
	Count 21	Count 22	Count 23	Count 24

Begin again.

Stroll Along ChaCha

Four wall dance. 32 counts
Music suggestion: Big Hair; Stroll Along
Choreographer: Rodeo Cowboys

Memory jogger

Counts 1–8: Step across, rock back, ChaCha. Repeat
Counts 9–24: Step across, side, behind, side, step across, rock back, ChaCha. Repeat
Counts 25–28: Pivot ½ ChaCha
Counts 29–32: Pivot ¼ ChaCha

Description with foot patterns

Counts 1–8: Step across, rock back, ChaCha. Repeat

Step across, rock back (on the spot)	Step L foot diagonally forward across R foot. Count 1	Rock back to R foot. Count 2	
ChaCha (moving L)	Step L foot to side. Count 3	Step R foot towards L foot. Count &	Step L foot to side. Count 4

(Counts 5–8: Repeat counts 1–4 starting on R foot with ChaCha moving R)

Counts 9–24: Step across, side, behind, side, step across, rock back, ChaCha. Repeat

Step across, side, behind, side (moving R)	Step L foot across in front of R foot. Count 9	Step R foot to side. Count 10	Step L foot behind R foot. Count 11	Step R foot to side. Count 12
Step across, rock back (on the spot)	Step L foot diagonally forward across R foot. Count 13	Rock back to R foot. Count 14		
ChaCha (moving L)	Step L foot to side. Count 15	Step R foot towards L foot. Count &	Step L foot to side. Count 16	

(Counts 17–24: Repeat counts 9–16 starting R foot and moving L then R)

Counts 25–28: Pivot ½, ChaCha

Pivot ½ (tng R)	Step L foot forward tng ½ to Count 25	Replace weight forward to R foot. Count 26	
ChaCha (moving forward)	Step L foot forward. Count 27	Step R foot towards L foot. Count &	Step L foot forward. Count 28

Counts 29–32: Pivot ¼, ChaCha

Pivot ¼ (tng L)	Step R foot forward tng ¼ to	Replace weight forward to L foot.	
	Count 29	Count 30	
ChaCha (moving forward)	Step R foot forward.	Step L foot towards R foot.	Step R foot forward.
	Count 31	Count &	Count 32

Begin again.

Note: This can be danced as a partner dance.

Start in side by side position both facing same way. Hold both hands, R hands at head height. On the ½ pivot on count 25 allow R hands to lower and L hands to move to head height. On the ¼ pivot on count 29, release L hands. Lady will turn 1¼ to L under raised R hands. Take hold both hands to start again.

Heads or Tails

Two wall dance. 32 counts
Music suggestion: Heads Carolina, Tails California
Choreographer: Barbara J Mason, USA

Memory jogger

Counts 1–8: Dig, hook and shuffle R & L
Counts 9–16: Rock & recover, 3 times and 2 stomps
Counts 17–24: Kick, ball change and pivot turn. Repeat
Counts 25–32: Vine R with scuff, vine L with stomp

Description with foot patterns
Counts 1–8: Dig, hook and shuffle R & L

Dig, hook (on the spot)	Dig R heel forward.	Hook R heel over L leg.	
	Count 1	Count 2	
Shuffle R (moving R)	Step R foot to side.	Step L foot towards R foot.	Step R foot to side.
	Count 3	Count &	Count 4

(Counts 5–8: Repeat counts 1–4 starting L heel and moving L)

Counts 9–16: Rock & recover, 3 times and 2 stomps

Rock and recover 3 times and 2 stomps (on the spot)	Rock R foot forward.	Rock L foot back.	Rock R foot back.	Rock L foot forward.
	Count 9	Count 10	Count 11	Count 12
	Rock R foot forward.	Rock L foot back.	Stomp R foot forward.	Stomp L foot in place.
	Count 13	Count 14	Count 15	Count 16

Counts 17–24: Kick, ball change and pivot turn. Repeat

Kick, ball change (on the spot)	Kick R foot forward.	Rock R foot back.	Step L foot in place.
	Count 17	Count &	Count 18

Pivot turn (on the spot)	Step R foot forward pivoting ¼ to L.	Step L foot in place.	
	Count 19	**Count 20**	
Kick, ball change (on the spot)	Kick R foot forward.	Rock R foot back.	Step L foot in place.
	Count 21	**Count &**	**Count 22**
Pivot turn (on the spot)	Step R foot forward pivoting ¼ to L.	Step L foot in place.	
	Count 23	**Count 24**	

Counts 25–32: Vine R with scuff, vine L with stomp

Vine R with scuff (moving R)	Step R foot to side.	Cross L foot behind R foot.	Step R foot to side.	Scuff L foot next to R foot.
	Count 25	**Count 26**	**Count 27**	**Count 28**
Vine L with stomp (moving L)	Step L foot to side.	Cross R foot behind L foot.	Step L foot to side.	Stomp R foot next to L foot.
	Count 29	**Count 30**	**Count 31**	**Count 32**

Begin again.

Hooked On Country

Four wall dance. 32 counts
Music suggestion: Hooked on Country Part 1; And I Worry
Choreographer: Unknown

Memory jogger

Counts 1–12: R & L shuffles back, 3 walks forward, kick, 3 walks back
  and ball change
Counts 13–24: R & L vine with kicks, step kicks R & L
Counts 25–32: 2 heel digs & 2 toe taps, ¼ turn, side, stomp and kick

Description with foot patterns

Counts 1–12: R & L shuffles back, 3 walks forward, kick, 3 walks back and ball change

R shuffles back (moving back)	Step R foot back. Small step.	Close L foot towards R foot.	Step R foot back. Small step.	
	Count 1	Count &	Count 2	
L shuffles back (moving back)	Step L foot back. Small step.	Close R foot towards L foot.	Step L foot back. Small step.	
	Count 3	Count &	Count 4	
3 walks forward & kick (moving forward)	Step R foot forward.	Step L foot forward.	Step R foot forward.	Kick L foot forward and clap hands.
	Count 5	Count 6	Count 7	Count 8

3 walks back, ball change *(moving back)*	Step L foot back.	Step R foot back.	Step L foot back.	Step R foot back.
	Count 9	**Count 10**	**Count 11**	**Count &**
	Cross L foot over R foot.			
	Count 12			

Counts 13–24: R & L vine with kicks, step kicks R & L

Vine R and kick *(moving R)*	Step R foot to side.	Cross L foot behind R foot.	Step R foot to side.	Kick L foot across R leg and clap.
	Count 13	**Count 14**	**Count 15**	**Count 16**
Vine L and kick *(moving L)*	Step L foot to side.	Cross R foot behind L foot.	Step L foot to side.	Kick R foot across L leg and clap.
	Count 17	**Count 18**	**Count 19**	**Count 20**
Step kicks *(on the spot)*	Step R foot to side.	Kick L foot across R leg and clap.	Step L foot to side.	Kick R foot across L leg and clap.
	Count 21	**Count 22**	**Count 23**	**Count 24**

Counts 25–32: 2 heel digs and 2 toe taps, ¼ turn, side, stomp and kick

2 heel digs and 2 toe taps (on the spot)	Dig R heel forward.	Dig R heel forward.	Tap R toe back.	Tap R toe back.
	Count 25	**Count 26**	**Count 27**	**Count 28**
¼ turn, stomp and kick (moving forward then tng L)	Step R foot forward pivoting ¼ to L.	Step L foot to side.	Stomp R foot beside L foot without weight.	Kick R foot forward.
	Count 29	**Count 30**	**Count 31**	**Count 32**

Begin again.

Note: Start on the 13th beat of music after the change in tempo.

Cowboy Rhythm

Four wall dance. 48 counts
Music suggestion: Cowboy Rhythm; Baby Likes to Rock it
Choreographer: Jo Thompson

Memory jogger

Counts 1–8: Stomp and 3 toe taps. Repeat
Counts 9–16: Stomp R, L, 2 slaps and 2 hip bumps
Counts 17–24: Step, close, heel splits twice
Counts 25–32: Back, tap and clap 4 times
Counts 33–40: Vine and hitch R & L
Counts 41–48: Step forward and scuff repeated 4 times with ¼ turn to L

Description with foot patterns
Counts 1–8: Stomp and 3 toe taps. Repeat

Stomp R and 3 toe taps (forward then on the spot)	Stomp R foot forward with toe turned in and weight on heel.	Leaving R heel on floor tap R toe out.	Leaving R heel on floor tap R toe in.	Leaving R heel on floor tap R toe out now taking weight.
	Count 1	**Count 2**	**Count 3**	**Count 4**
Stomp L and 3 toe taps (forward then on the spot)	Stomp L foot forward with toe turned in and weight on heel.	Leaving L heel on floor tap L toe out.	Leaving L heel on floor tap L toe in.	Leaving L heel on floor tap L toe out now taking weight.
	Count 5	**Count 6**	**Count 7**	**Count 8**

Counts 9–16: Stomp R, L, 2 slaps and 2 hip bumps

2 stomps, 2 slaps and 2 hip bumps (on the spot)	Stomp R foot forward and slightly to side.	Stomp L foot forward and slightly to side.	Lift R foot behind L knee and slap with L hand.	Step R foot to side.
	Count 9	**Count 10**	**Count 11**	**Count 12**
	Lift L foot behind R knee and slap with R hand.	Step L foot to side.	Hip bump to R clapping hands.	Hip bump to L clapping hands.
	Count 13	**Count 14**	**Count 15**	**Count 16**

Counts 17–24: Step, close, heel splits twice

Step, close, *heel splits* *(forward then on the spot)*	Step R foot diagonally forward.	Close L foot to R foot.	Fan both heels out leaving toes together. Click fingers.	Fan both heels in together. Click fingers.
	Count 17	*Count 18*	*Count 19*	*Count 20*
	Step L foot diagonally forward.	Close R foot to L foot.	Fan both heels out leaving toes together. Click fingers.	Fan both heels in together. Click fingers.
	Count 21	*Count 22*	*Count 23*	*Count 24*

Counts 25–32: Back, tap and clap 4 times

Back steps *with taps &* *claps* *(moving back)*	Step R foot back tng body to R.	Tap L foot to R foot, clapping hands.	Step L foot back tng body to L.	Tap R foot to L foot, clapping hands.
	Count 25	*Count 26*	*Count 27*	*Count 28*
	Step R foot back tng body to R.	Tap L foot to R foot, clapping hands.	Step L foot back tng body to L.	Tap R foot to L foot, clapping hands.
	Count 29	*Count 30*	*Count 31*	*Count 32*

Counts 33–40: Vine and hitch R & L

Vine R and hitch (moving R)	Step R foot to side slapping hands on outside of thighs.	Cross L foot behind R foot slapping hands on ouside of thighs.	Step R foot to side clapping hands.	Hitch L knee snapping fingers.
	Count 33	Count 34	Count 35	Count 36
Vine L and hitch (moving L)	Step L foot to side slapping hands on outside of thighs.	Cross R foot behind L foot slapping hands on outside of thighs.	Step L foot to side clapping hands.	Hitch R knee snapping fingers.
	Count 37	Count 38	Count 39	Count 40

Counts 41–48: Step forward and scuff repeated 4 times with ¼ turn to L

Step forward and scuff twice (moving forward)	Step R foot forward.	Scuff L heel forward.	Step L foot forward.	Scuff R heel forward.
	Count 41	Count 42	Count 43	Count 44
Step forward, scuff twice tng ¼ L (moving forward then tng L)	Step R foot forward.	Scuff L heel forward.	Step L foot forward.	Scuff R heel forward tng ¼ to L.
	Count 45	Count 46	Count 47	Count 48

Begin again.

Cajun Skip (sometimes known as The Skip)

Two wall dance. 20 counts
Music suggestion: Cajun Strut
Choreographer: Unknown

Memory jogger

Counts 1–8: Vine L with hitch, vine R tng R with hitch tng ¼ to R
Counts 9–16: Rock L, R, L with hitch tng ½ L, rock R, L, R hitch tng ¼ R
Counts 17–20: Step L hitch tng ¼ R, step R hitch tng ¼ R

Description with foot patterns

Counts 1–8: Vine L with hitch, vine R tng R with hitch tng ¼ to R

| **Vine L with hitch** (moving L) | Step L foot to side. Count 1 | Cross R foot behind L foot. Count 2 | Step L foot to side. Count 3 | Hitch R knee. Count 4 |
| **Vine R with hitch tng R** (moving R then tng R) | Step R foot to side. Count 5 | Cross L foot behind R foot. Count 6 | Step R foot to side tng ¼ to R. Count 7 | Hitch L knee. Count 8 |

Counts 9–16: Rock L, R, L with hitch tng ½ L, rock R, L, R hitch tng ¼ R

| **Rock L, R, L with hitch tng ½ L** (on the spot then tng L) | Rock L foot forward. Count 9 | Rock R foot back. Count 10 | Rock L foot forward. Count 11 | Hitch R knee tng ½ to L. Count 12 |

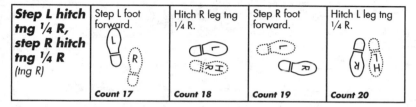

Rock R, L, R with hitch tng ¼ R (on the spot then tng R)	Rock R foot forward.	Rock L foot back.	Rock R foot forward.	Hitch L knee tng ¼ to R.
	Count 13	Count 14	Count 15	Count 16

Counts 17–20: Step L hitch tng ¼ R, step R hitch tng ¼ R

Step L hitch tng ¼ R, step R hitch tng ¼ R (tng R)	Step L foot forward.	Hitch R leg tng ¼ R.	Step R foot forward.	Hitch L leg tng ¼ R.
	Count 17	Count 18	Count 19	Count 20

Begin again.

Level 7 dance charts

Grundy Gallop

Two wall dance. 32 counts
Music suggestion: Sold; Heart made of Stone

Memory jogger

Counts 1–8: 4 shuffle steps tng full circle to L
Counts 9–12: Side touches L and R
Counts 13–20: Heel, toe and shuffles L and R
Counts 21–28: Rock forward, back, shuffle back, rock back, forward, shuffle forward
Counts 29–32: Step L and turn, stomp, stomp

Description with foot patterns
Counts 1–8: 4 shuffle steps tng full circle to L

4 shuffles tng full circle *(tng L)*	Step L foot forward tng L.	Step R foot towards L foot still tng L.	Step L foot forward tng L. ¼ turn to L over counts 1 & 2.	Step R foot forward tng L.
	Count 1	**Count &**	**Count 2**	**Count 3**
	Step L foot towards R foot still tng L.	Step R foot forward tng L. ¼ turn to L over counts 3 & 4.	Step L foot forward tng L.	Step R foot towards L foot still tng L.
	Count &	**Count 4**	**Count 5**	**Count &**
	Step L foot forward tng L. ¼ turn to L over counts 5 & 6.	Step R foot forward tng L.	Step L foot towards R foot still tng L.	Step R foot forward tng L. ¼ turn to L over counts 7 & 8.
	Count 6	**Count 7**	**Count &**	**Count 8**

Counts 9–12: Side touches L & R

L side point and R side point *(on the spot)*	Point L toe to side.	Close L foot to R foot.	Point R toe to side.	Close R foot to L foot.
	Count 9	**Count 10**	**Count 11**	**Count 12**

Counts 13–20: Heel, toe and shuffles L & R

Dig, point and shuffle twice *(on the spot then forward twice)*	Dig L heel forward.	Point L toe back.	Step L foot forward.	Step R foot towards L foot.
	Count 13	**Count 14**	**Count 15**	**Count &**

	Step L foot forward.	Dig R heel forward.	Point R toe back.	Step R foot forward.
	L R	D R	L P R	R L
	Count 16	**Count 17**	**Count 18**	**Count 19**
	Step L foot towards R foot.	Step R foot forward.		
	R L	R L		
	Count &	**Count 20**		

Counts 21–28: Rock forward, back, shuffle back, rock back, forward, shuffle forward

Rock, rock & shuffle twice *(on the spot and back then on the spot and forward)*	Rock L foot forward.	Rock R foot back.	Step L foot back.	Step R foot towards L foot.
	L R	L R	R L	R L
	Count 21	**Count 22**	**Count 23**	**Count &**
	Step L foot back.	Rock R foot back.	Rock L foot forward.	Step R foot forward.
	R L	L R	L R	R L
	Count 24	**Count 25**	**Count 26**	**Count 27**
	Step L foot towards R foot.	Step R foot forward.		
	R L	R L		
	Count &	**Count 28**		

Counts 29–32: Step L and turn, stomp, stomp

Step L and turn, stomp, stomp (tng R then on the spot)	Step L foot forward pivoting ½ turn to R.	Replace weight to R foot.	Stomp L foot next to R foot.	Stomp R foot in place.
	Count 29	Count 30	Count 31	Count 32

Begin again.

Running Bear

One wall dance. 96 counts
Music suggestion: Running Bear
Choreographer: Neil Hale

Memory jogger

Counts 1–32: 4 toe struts, rock, rock, shuffles back, rock, rock. Repeat

Counts 33–64: Crossing toe strut, side toe strut, rock, rock and side shuffle. Repeat dancing a stomp instead of a side shuffle

Counts 65–96: 2 sailor shuffles, forward shuffles, 2 heel digs, pivot and 2 stomps. Repeat

Description with foot patterns

Counts 1–32: 4 toe struts, rock, rock, shuffles back, rock, rock. Repeat

Toe struts (moving forward)	Step R toe forward.	Drop R heel to take weight.	Step L toe forward.	Drop L heel to take weight.
	Count 1	Count 2	Count 3	Count 4
	Step R toe forward.	Drop R heel to take weight.	Step L toe forward.	Drop L heel to take weight.
	Count 5	Count 6	Count 7	Count 8

Rock shuffles back, rock, (on the spot, moving back then on the spot)	Rock R foot forward.	Rock L foot back.	Step R foot back.	Step L foot towards R foot.
	Count 9	**Count 10**	**Count 11**	**Count &**
	Step R foot back.	Step L foot back.	Step R foot towards L foot.	Step L foot back.
	Count 12	**Count 13**	**Count &**	**Count 14**
	Rock R foot back.	Rock L foot forward.		
	Count 15	**Count 16**		

(Counts 17–32: Repeat counts 1–16.)

Counts 33–64: Crossing toe strut, side toe strut, rock, rock and side shuffle. Repeat dancing a stomp instead of a side shuffle

Crossing toe strut, side toe strut (moving L)	Step R toe across L foot.	Drop R heel to take weight.	Step L toe to side.	Drop L heel to take weight.
	Count 33	**Count 34**	**Count 35**	**Count 36**
Rock, rock and side shuffle (on the spot then moving R)	Step R foot behind L foot.	Rock L foot forward.	Step R foot to side.	Close L foot towards R foot.
	Count 37	**Count 38**	**Count 39**	**Count &**

	Step R foot to side. **Count 40**			
Crossing toe strut, side toe strut *(moving R)*	Step L toe across R foot. **Count 41**	Drop L heel to take weight. **Count 42**	Step R toe to side. **Count 43**	Drop R heel to take weight. **Count 44**
Rock, rock and side shuffle *(on the spot then moving L)*	Step L foot behind R foot. **Count 45**	Rock R foot forward. **Count 46**	Step L foot to side. **Count 47**	Close R foot towards L foot. **Count &**
	Step L foot to side. **Count 48**			
Crossing toe strut, side toe strut *(moving L)*	Step R toe across L foot. **Count 49**	Drop R heel to take weight. **Count 50**	Step L toe to side. **Count 51**	Drop L heel to take weight. **Count 52**
Rock, rock and side shuffle *(on the spot then moving R)*	Step R foot behind L foot. **Count 53**	Rock L foot forward. **Count 54**	Step R foot to side. **Count 55**	Close L foot towards R foot. **Count &**

	Step R foot to side. **Count 56**			
Crossing toe strut, side toe strut *(moving R)*	Step L toe across R foot. **Count 57**	Drop L heel to take weight. **Count 58**	Step R toe to side. **Count 59**	Drop R heel to take weight. **Count 60**
Rock, rock, stomp *(on the spot)*	Step L foot behind R foot. **Count 61**	Rock R foot forward. **Count 62**	Stomp L foot to side. Hold for one count. **Count 63, 64**	

Counts 65–96: 2 sailor shuffles, forward shuffles, 2 heel digs, pivot and 2 stomps. Repeat.

Sailor shuffles *(on the spot)*	Cross R foot behind L foot. **Count 65**	Step L foot to side. **Count &**	Step R foot in place. **Count 66**
Sailor shuffles *(on the spot)*	Cross L foot behind R foot. **Count 67**	Step R foot to side. **Count &**	Step L foot in place. **Count 68**
Forward shuffle *(moving forward)*	Step R foot forward. **Count 69**	Move L foot towards R foot. **Count &**	Step R foot forward. **Count 70**

Forward shuffle *(moving forward)*	Step L foot forward. **Count 71**	Move R foot towards L foot. **Count &**	Step L foot forward. **Count 72**	
2 heel digs *(on the spot)*	Dig R heel forward. **Count 73**	Close R foot to L foot. **Count 74**	Dig L heel forward. **Count 75**	Close L foot to R foot. **Count 76**
Pivot and stomps *(tng L then moving forward)*	Step R foot forward pivoting ½ turn to L. **Count 77**	Step L foot forward. **Count 78**	Stomp R foot forward. **Count 79**	Stomp L foot forward. **Count 80**
Sailor shuffles *(on the spot)*	Cross R foot behind L foot. **Count 81**	Step L foot to side. **Count &**	Step R foot in place. **Count 82**	
Sailor shuffles *(on the spot)*	Cross L foot behind R foot. **Count 83**	Step R foot to side. **Count &**	Step L foot in place. **Count 84**	
Forward shuffle *(moving forward)*	Step R foot forward. **Count 85**	Move L foot towards R foot. **Count &**	Step R foot forward. **Count 86**	

Forward shuffle *(moving forward)*	Step L foot forward. Count 87	Move R foot towards L foot. Count &	Step L foot forward. Count 88	
2 heel digs *(on the spot)*	Dig R heel forward. Count 89	Close R foot to L foot. Count 90	Dig L heel forward. Count 91	Close L foot to R foot. Count 92
Pivot and stomps *(tng L then moving forward)*	Step R foot forward pivoting ½ turn to L. Count 93	Step L foot forward. Count 94	Stomp R foot forward. Count 95	Stomp L foot forward. Count 96

Begin again.

Note: The dance is choreographed to phase to 'Running Bear' by The Dean Brothers. The whole sequence should be danced through three times and then counts 65–96 danced again.

Wrangler Butts

Four wall dance. 32 counts
Music suggestion: Wrangler Butts
Choreographer: Rodeo Ruth

Memory jogger

Counts 1–8: Stepping out and in, 4 knee pops
Counts 9–16: Vine R with ¼ turn, forward L, slide, forward and touch
Counts 17–24: Vine R, L shimmy and clap
Counts 25–32: 2 step pivots, toe touches R, L, R and touch

Description with foot patterns
Counts 1–8: Stepping out and in, 4 knee pops

Stepping out and in (on the spot)	Step R foot to side. Slap R hand on R buttock.	Step L foot to side. Slap L hand on L buttock.	Step R foot in and slap R hand on R front pocket.	Step L foot in and slap L hand on L front pocket.
	Count 1	Count 2	Count 3	Count 4
Knee pops (on the spot)	Lift L heel and push L knee forward.	Lower L heel and lift R heel pushing R knee forward.	Lower R heel and lift L heel pushing L knee forward.	Lower L heel and lift R heel pushing R knee forward.
	Count 5	Count 6	Count 7	Count 8

Counts 9–16: Vine R with ¼ turn, forward L, slide, forward and touch

Vine R with ¼ turn (moving R then tng L)	Step R foot to side.	Cross L foot behind R foot.	Step R foot to side making ¼ turn to L.	Touch L toe beside R foot.
	Count 9	Count 10	Count 11	Count 12
Camel walks (moving forward)	Step L foot forward.	Slide R foot beside L foot taking weight.	Step L foot forward.	Slide R foot beside L foot and touch.
	Count 13	Count 14	Count 15	Count 16

Counts 17–24: Vine R, L shimmy and clap

Vine R (moving R)	Step R foot to side.	Cross L foot behind R foot.	Step R foot to side.	Touch L foot beside R foot.
	Count 17	**Count 18**	**Count 19**	**Count 20**
L shimmy (moving L)	Step L foot making large step to side.	Shimmy for two counts as you slide-up R foot next to L foot.	Clap hands.	
	Count 21	**Count 22,23**	**Count 24**	

Counts 25–32: 2 step pivots, toe touches R, L, R and touch

Step pivots (forward then tng L)	Step R foot forward pivoting ¼ turn to L.	Step L foot forward swinging hips R and L.	Step R foot forward pivoting ¼ turn to L.	Step L foot forward swinging hips R and L.
	Count 25	**Count 26**	**Count 27**	**Count 28**
Toes touches (on the spot)	Touch R toe to side.	Step R foot beside L foot.	Touch L toe to side.	Step L foot beside R foot.
	Count 29	**Count &**	**Count 30**	**Count &**
	Touch R toe to side.	Touch R toe beside L foot.		
	Count 31	**Count 32**		

Begin again.

Note: Begin dance on vocals.

Ribbon of Highway

One wall dance. 64 counts
Music suggestion: Ribbon of Highway
Choreographer: Neil Hale

Memory jogger

Counts 1–8: Side, hold, close, hold, right chasse and hold
Counts 9–16: Side, hold, close, hold, left chasse and hold
Counts 17–24: Slow forward coaster step, back steps with holds
Counts 25–32: Slow back coaster step, forward steps with holds
Counts 33–40: Rock steps and holds, back ¼ turn, together, ¼ turn, hold
Counts 41–48: Rock steps and holds, back ¼ turn, together ¼ turn, hold
Counts 49–56: Step, pivot and holds, ¼ turn, together, ¼ turn and hold
Counts 57–64: Heel digs and toe tap

Description with foot patterns
Counts 1–8: Side, hold, close, hold, right chasse and hold

Side, hold, close, hold (moving R)	Step R foot to side. Hold for one count.	Close L foot to R foot. Hold for one count.	
	Count 1, 2	***Count 3, 4***	
Chasse and hold (moving R)	Step R foot to side (small step).	Close L foot to R foot.	Step R foot to side (small step). Hold for one count.
	Count 5	***Count 6***	***Count 7, 8***

Counts 9–16: Side, hold, close, hold, left chasse and hold

Side, hold, close, hold (moving L)	Step L foot to side. Hold for one count.	Close R foot to L foot. Hold for one count.	
	L R	L R	
	Count 9, 10	**Count 11, 12**	
Chasse and hold (moving L)	Step L foot to side (small step).	Close R foot to L foot.	Step L foot to side (small step). Hold for one count.
	L R	L R	L R
	Count 13	**Count 14**	**Count 15, 16**

Counts 17–24: Slow forward coaster step, back steps with holds

Slow forward coaster step (forward and back)	Step R foot forward.	Close L foot next to R foot.	Step R foot back. Hold for one count.
	R L	L R	L R
	Count 17	**Count 18**	**Count 19, 20**
Back steps with holds (moving back)	Step L foot back. Hold for one count.	Step R foot back. Hold for one count.	
	R L	L R	
	Count 21, 22	**Count 23, 24**	

Counts 25–32: Slow back coaster step, forward steps with holds

Slow back coaster step (back and forward)	Step L foot back. Count 25	Close R foot next to L foot. Count 26	Step L foot forward. Hold for one count. Count 27, 28
Forward steps with holds (moving forward)	Step R foot forward. Hold for one count. Count 29, 30	Step L foot forward. Hold for one count. Count 31, 32	

Counts 33–40: Rock steps and holds, back ¼ turn, together, ¼ turn, hold

Rock steps and holds (on the spot)	Rock R foot forward. Hold for one count. Count 33, 34	Rock L foot back. Hold for one count. Count 35, 36	
Back ¼ turn, close, side ¼ turn (tng R)	Step R foot back tng ¼ to R. Count 37	Close L foot to R foot. Count 38	Step R foot to side tng ¼ to R. Hold for one count. Count 39, 40

Counts 41–48: Rock steps and holds, back ¼ turn, together ¼ turn, hold

Rock steps and holds (on the spot)	Rock L foot forward. Hold for one count.	Rock R foot back. Hold for one count.	
	Count 41, 42	Count 43, 44	
Back ¼ turn, close, side ¼ turn (tng L)	Step L foot back tng ¼ to L.	Close R foot to L foot.	Step L foot to side tng ¼ to L. Hold for one count.
	Count 45	Count 46	Count 47, 48

Counts 49–56: Step, pivot and holds, ¼ turn, together, ¼ turn and hold

Step, pivot and holds (tng to L)	Step R foot forward. Hold for one count.	Pivot ½ to L putting weight on L foot. Hold for one count.	
	Count 49, 50	Count 51, 52	
¼ turn, close, ¼ turn and hold (tng to L)	Step R foot forward tng ¼ L.	Close L foot to R foot.	Step R foot forward tng ¼ L. Hold for one count.
	Count 53	Count 54	Count 55, 56

Note: Steps 53–56 are done in a tight circle with small steps

Counts 57–64: Heel digs and toe tap

Heel digs (on the spot)	Dig L heel forward.	Close L foot to R foot.	Dig R heel forward.	Close R foot to L foot.
	Count 57	Count 58	Count 59	Count 60
Heel dig and toe tap (tng to L then moving forward)	Dig L heel forward.	Close L foot to R foot.	Tap R toe next to L toe. Hold for one count.	
	Count 61	Count 62	Count 63, 64	

Begin again.

Black Coffee

Four wall dance. 44 counts
Music suggestion: Black Coffee
Choreographer: Helen O'Malley

Memory jogger

Counts 1–12: Kick twice and shuffle R & L and 2 paddle turns
Counts 13–24: Rock forward, back and shuffle R & L with turn, switches
Counts 25–36: Side, close twice R with shoulder shimmies and claps, vine L with scuff
Counts 37–48: Side, cross behind, side, cross in front with finger clicks, pivot turns

Description with foot patterns
Counts 1–12: Kick twice and shuffle R & L and 2 paddle turns

Kicks, shuffles (on the spot)	Kick R foot forward.	Kick R foot forward again.	Step R foot to side (small step).	Move L foot towards R foot.
	Count 1	Count 2	Count 3	Count &

	Step R foot to side (small step).	Kick L foot forward.	Kick L foot forward again.	Step L foot to side (small step).
	Count 4	**Count 5**	**Count 6**	**Count 7**
	Move R foot towards L foot.	Step L foot to side (small step).		
	Count &	**Count 8**		
Paddle turns *(moving L)*	Tap R toe forward with some weight tng ⅛ to L.	Step L foot in place.	Tap R toe forward with some weight tng ⅛ to L.	Step L foot in place.
	Count 9	**Count 10**	**Count 11**	**Count 12**

Counts 13–24: Rock forward, back and shuffle R & L with turn, switches

	Rock R foot forward.	Rock L foot back.	Step R foot to side (small step) beginning to turn R.	Move L foot towards R foot still tng to R.
Rock, shuffles with ½ turn twice *(on the spot then to R, on the spot then to L)*	**Count 13**	**Count 14**	**Count 15**	**Count &**
	Step R foot to side (small step) still tng to R. (½ turn to R over counts 15 & 16).	Rock L foot forward.	Rock R foot back.	Step L foot to side (small step) beginning to turn L.
	Count 16	**Count 17**	**Count 18**	**Count 19**

	Move R foot towards L foot still tng to L. **Count &**	Step L foot to side (small step) still tng to L. (½ turn to L over counts 19 & 20) **Count 20**	
Switches *(on the spot)*	Dig R heel forward. **Count 21**	Replace R foot to its place digging L heel forward. **Count 22**	Replace L foot to its place digging R heel forward. **Count 23**	Hold position and clap hands. **Count 24**

Counts 25–36: Side, close twice R with shoulder shimmies and claps, vine L with scuff

Side steps R with shoulder shimmies *(moving R)*	Step R foot to side shimmying shoulders. **Count 25**	Hold for one count. **Count 26**	Close L foot to R foot. **Count 27**	Hold for one count and clap. **Count 28**
	Step R foot to side shimmying shoulders. **Count 29**	Hold for one count. **Count 30**	Close L foot to R foot. **Count 31**	Hold for one count, changing weight to R foot and clap. **Count 32**
Vine L with scuff *(moving L)*	Step L foot to side. **Count 33**	Cross R foot behind L foot. **Count 34**	Step L foot to side. **Count 35**	Scuff R foot next to L foot. **Count 36**

Counts 37–48: Side, cross behind, side, cross in front with finger clicks, pivot turns

Side, crosses (moving R)	Step R foot to side.	Hold position while clicking fingers at shoulder height.	Cross L foot behind R foot.	Hold position while clicking fingers behind hips.
	Count 37	**Count 38**	**Count 39**	**Count 40**
	Step R foot to side.	Hold position while clicking fingers at shoulder height.	Cross L foot in front of R foot.	Hold position while clicking fingers behind hips.
	Count 41	**Count 42**	**Count 43**	**Count 44**
Pivot turns (moving L)	Step R foot forward then pivot ½ L to face opposite wall.	Step L foot forward.	Step R foot forward then pivot ½ R to face opposite wall.	Step L foot forward.
	Count 45	**Count 46**	**Count 47**	**Count 48**

Begin again.

All Aboard

Four wall dance. 32 counts
Music suggestion: My Baby Thinks She's A Train
Choreographer: Max Perry & Jo Thompson

Memory jogger

Counts 1–8: Rock forward, back, forward, and coaster step starting R
Counts 9–16: Rock forward, back, forward, and coaster step starting L
Counts 17–24: Cross, side (3 times) and cross, cross, side, behind, forward
    with turn, forward
Counts 25–32: 2 pivot turns and 4 chug walks

Description with foot patterns

Counts 1–8: Rock forward, back, forward, and coaster step starting R

Rock steps *(on the spot)*	Rock R heel forward.	Step L foot in place.	Rock R toe back.	Step L foot in place.
	Count 1	*Count 2*	*Count 3*	*Count 4*
	Rock R heel forward.	Step L foot in place.		
	Count 5	*Count 6*		
Coaster step *(on the spot)*	Step R foot back.	Step L foot to R foot.	Step R foot forward.	
	Count 7	*Count &*	*Count 8*	

Counts 9–16: Rock forward, back, forward, and coaster step starting L

Rock steps *(on the spot)*	Rock L heel forward.	Step R foot in place.	Rock L toe back.	Step R foot in place.
	Count 9	*Count 10*	*Count 11*	*Count 12*
	Rock L heel forward.	Step R foot in place.		
	Count 13	*Count 14*		

Coaster step (on the spot)	Step L foot back. 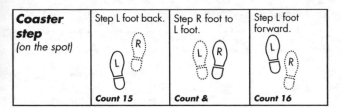 Count 15	Step R foot to L foot. Count &	Step L foot forward. Count 16

Counts 17–24: Cross, side (3 times) and cross, cross, side, behind, forward with turn, forward

Cross, side 3 times and cross (moving L)	Cross R foot over L foot. Count 17	Step L foot to side and slightly back. Count &	Cross R foot over L foot. Count 18	Step L foot to side and slightly back. Count &
	Cross R foot over L foot. Count 19	Step L foot to side and slightly back. Count &	Cross R foot over L foot. Count 20	
Cross, side behind, side tng R, forward (moving R then tng R)	Cross L foot over R foot. Count 21	Step R foot to side. Count 22	Cross L foot behind R foot. Count 23	Step R foot forward making ¼ turn to R. Count &
	Step L foot forward. Count 24			

Counts 25–32: 2 pivot turns and 4 chug walks

Pivot turns (tng L)	Step R foot forward pivoting ½ to L.	Step L foot forward.	Step R foot forward pivoting ½ to L.	Step L foot forward.
	Count 25	*Count 26*	*Count 27*	*Count 28*
Chug walks (moving forward)	Step R foot forward. Slide-up L toe next to it.	Step L foot forward. Slide-up R toe next to it.	Step R foot forward. Slide-up L toe next to it.	Step L foot forward. Slide-up R toe next to it.
	Count 29	*Count 30*	*Count 31*	*Count 32*

Begin again.

Note: Counts 29–32 can be danced as forward walks.

Tush Push

Four wall dance. 40 counts
Music suggestion: Backtrack
Choreographer: Jim & Martie Ferrazzanno

Memory jogger

Counts 1–12: Dig, close, dig, dig, R & L, 3 switches and clap
Counts 13–20: Hip bumps R, R, L, L, R, L, R, L
Counts 21–36: Shuffle rock forward, shuffle rock back, shuffle and turn twice
Counts 37–40: Step, turn, stomp and clap

Description with foot patterns

Counts 1–12: Dig, close, dig, dig, R & L, 3 switches and clap

Digs, switches and clap (on the spot)	Dig R heel forward.	Step R foot in place without weight.	Dig R heel forward.	Dig R heel forward.
	Count 1	**Count 2**	**Count 3**	**Count 4**
	Bring R foot back in place and at same time dig L heel forward.	Step L foot in place without weight.	Dig L heel forward.	Dig L heel forward.
	Count 5	**Count 6**	**Count 7**	**Count 8**
	Bring L foot back in place and at same time dig R heel forward.	Bring R foot back in place and at same time dig L heel forward.	Bring L foot back in place and at same time dig R heel forward.	Hold position and clap hands.
	Count 9	**Count 10**	**Count 11**	**Count 12**

Counts 13–20: Hip bumps R, R, L, L, R, L, R, L

Hip bumps (on the spot)	Bump R hip forward twice.	Bump L hip back twice.	Bump R hip forward.	Bump L hip back.
	Count 13, 14	**Count 15, 16**	**Count 17**	**Count 18**
	Bump R hip forward.	Bump L hip back.		
	Count 19	**Count 20**		

Counts 21–36: Shuffle rock forward, shuffle rock back, shuffle and turn twice

Shuffles and rocks *(forward and back)*	Step R foot forward. Count 21	Step L foot towards R foot. Count &	Step R foot forward. Count 22	Step L foot forward. Count 23
	Rock R foot back. Count 24	Step L foot back. Count 25	Step R foot towards L foot. Count &	Step L foot back. Count 26
	Step R foot back. Count 27	Rock L foot forward. Count 28		
Shuffles and turns *(forward, turn R, forward and turn L)*	Step R foot forward. Count 29	Step L foot towards R foot. Count &	Step R foot forward. Count 30	Step L foot forward pivoting ½ to R. Count 31
	Step R foot forward. Count 32	Step L foot forward. Count 33	Step R foot towards L foot. Count &	Step L foot forward. Count 34
	Step R foot forward pivoting ½ to L. Count 35	Step L foot forward. Count 36		

Counts 37–40: Step, turn, stomp and clap

Forward tng, side, stomp and clap (forward turn L then on the spot)	Step R foot forward pivoting ¼ to L.	Step L foot to side.	Stomp R foot next to L foot without weight.	Hold position and clap hands.
	Count 37	**Count 38**	**Count 39**	**Count 40**

Begin again.

Note: There are many variations to this dance. Three are listed below.

Variation 1

Instead of the foot closes on counts 2 and 6, toe points or heel digs are sometimes danced.

Variation 2

To avoid the quick change on count 5, the first 8 counts are sometimes danced:

    1 Dig R heel forward.

    2 Close R foot to L foot.

    3 Dig R heel forward.

    4 Close R foot to L foot.

    5 Dig L heel forward.

    6 Close L foot to R foot.

    7 Dig L heel forward.

    8 Close L foot to R foot.

To avoid the quick change on counts 9, 10 and 11 these counts are sometimes danced:

    9 Twist R.

  10 Twist L.

  11 Twist centre.

  12 Step R foot forward and clap hands.

Variation 3

A hip roll moving clockwise can be danced on counts 17–20 instead of hip bumps.

Honky Tonk Twist II (also known as Twisting the Night Away)

Four wall dance. 64 counts
Music suggestion: Twisting the Night Away
Choreographer: Max Perry, USA

Memory jogger

Counts 1–16: Heel swivel R, centre, R, centre and R hooks, repeat L
Counts 17–24: Step forward, scuff, L and R, stroll back L, R, L and close
Counts 25–32: Swivel heels, toes, heels, toes, L then toes, heels, toes, heels, R
Counts 33–40: Monterey turn, toe struts back R & L
Counts 41–48: Hand jive, thighs twice, clap twice, hitch-hike R & L twice each
Counts 49–56: 2 heel struts, forward tng ¼ turn L
Counts 57–64: Jazz box, swivel heels L, centre, L, centre

Descriptions with foot patterns

Counts 1–16: Heel swivel R, centre, R, centre and R hooks, repeat L

Heel swivels (on the spot)	Swivel both heels to R.	Swivel both heels to centre.	Swivel both heels to R.	Swivel both heels to centre.
	Count 1	**Count 2**	**Count 3**	**Count 4**
Heel hooks (on the spot)	Take weight on L foot. Dig R heel forward.	Hook R heel in front of L knee.	Dig R heel forward.	Close R foot to L foot taking weight.
	Count 5	**Count 6**	**Count 7**	**Count 8**
Heel swivels (on the spot)	Swivel both heels to L.	Swivel both heels to centre.	Swivel both heels to L.	Swivel both heels to centre.
	Count 9	**Count 10**	**Count 11**	**Count 12**

Heel hooks (on the spot)	Take weight on R foot. Dig L heel forward.	Hook L heel in front of R knee.	Dig L heel forward.	Close L foot to R foot without weight.
	Count 13	Count 14	Count 15	Count 16

Counts 17–24: Step forward, scuff, L and R, stroll back L, R, L and close

Step, scuff, forward (moving forward)	Step L foot forward.	Scuff R foot next to L foot.	Step R foot forward.	Scuff L foot next to R foot.
	Count 17	Count 18	Count 19	Count 20
Stroll back (moving back)	Step L foot back.	Step R foot back.	Step L foot back.	Close R foot next to L foot.
	Count 21	Count 22	Count 23	Count 24

Counts 25–32: Swivel heels, toes, heels, toes, L then toes, heels, toes, heels, R

Heel and toe swivel (moving L then R)	Swivel both heels to L.	Swivel both toes to L.	Swivel both heels to L.	Swivel both toes to L.
	Count 25	Count 26	Count 27	Count 28
	Swivel both toes to R.	Swivel both heels to R.	Swivel both toes to R.	Swivel both heels to R.
	Count 29	Count 30	Count 31	Count 32

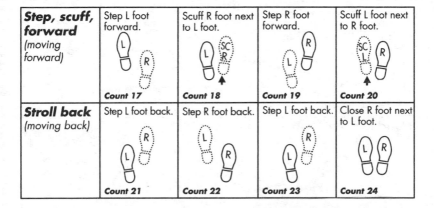

Counts 33–40: Monterey turn, toe struts back R & L

Monterey turn *(on the spot, tng R then on the spot)*	Point R toe out to side.	Pivot ½ turn R placing R foot next to L foot.	Point L toe to side.	Close L foot to R foot.
	Count 33	**Count 34**	**Count 35**	**Count 36**
Toe struts *(moving back)*	Step R foot back on ball of foot.	Lower R heel.	Step L foot back on ball of foot.	Lower L heel.
	Count 37	**Count 38**	**Count 39**	**Count 40**

Counts 41–48: Hand jive, thighs twice, clap twice, hitch-hike R & L twice each

Hand jive *(on the spot)*	Slap both hands on thighs twice.	Clap hands twice chest height.	Hitch-hike motion with R arm twice.	Hitch-hike motion with L arm twice.
	Count 41, 42	**Count 43, 44**	**Count 45, 46**	**Count 47, 48**

Counts 49–56: 2 heel struts, forward tng ¼ turn L

Heel struts *(moving forward)*	Step R heel forward.	Lower R toes to floor.	Step L heel forward.	Lower L toes to floor.
	Count 49	**Count 50**	**Count 51**	**Count 52**
Forward and turn ¼ to L *(moving forward then tng L)*	Step R foot forward.	Hold position.	Turn ¼ to L on ball of R foot. Step L foot to side.	Hold position.
	Count 53	**Count 54**	**Count 55**	**Count 56**

Counts 57–64: Jazz box, swivel heels L, centre, L, centre

Jazz box (on the spot)	Cross R foot over L foot.	Step L foot back.	Step R foot to side.	Step L foot next to R foot.
	Count 57	**Count 58**	**Count 59**	**Count 60**
Swivels (on the spot)	Swivel both heels to L.	Swivel both heels to centre.	Swivel both heels to L.	Swivel both heels to centre.
	Count 61	**Count 62**	**Count 63**	**Count 64**

Begin again.

Partner Dances

Western Barn Dance

Couples dance in circle. 28 counts
Music suggestion: Rock My World; Western Express
Choreographer: Unknown

Memory jogger

Begin in double hold (R hand holds partner's L hand, L hand holds partner's R hand).
Leader faces wall and partner.
Leader's steps given, partner's exact opposite unless stated.

Counts 1–8: Side L, close, side, tap, side R, close, side, tap
Counts 9–16: Repeat above with partner tng to R under leader's L arm
Counts 17–20: Turning to side by side position, both facing LOD, step L, scuff, R, scuff
Counts 21–28: Release hold, vine L to centre, then R to partner (Partner–vine R to wall then vine L back to partner)

Description with foot patterns

Counts 1–8: Side L, close, side, tap, side R, close, side tap

Side L, close, side tap (moving anti-clockwise)	Step L foot to side.	Close R foot to L foot.	Step L foot to side.	Tap R foot to L foot.
	Count 1	Count 2	Count 3	Count 4
Side R, close, side tap (moving clockwise)	Step R foot to side.	Close L foot to R foot.	Step R foot to side.	Tap L foot to R foot.
	Count 5	Count 6	Count 7	Count 8

Counts 9–16: Repeat counts 1–8 with partner tng to R under leader's L arm

Side L, close, side tap, tng partner (moving anti-clockwise)	Step L foot to side tng partner to R under L arm. Release R hand.	Close R foot to L foot still tng partner.	Step L foot to side still tng partner.	Tap R foot to L foot.
	Count 9	Count 10	Count 11	Count 12
Side R, close, side tap, tng partner (moving clockwise)	Step R foot to side tng partner to L under L arm.	Close L foot to R foot still tng partner.	Step R foot to side still tng partner.	Tap L foot to R foot.
	Count 13	Count 14	Count 15	Count 16

Counts 17–20: Taking side by side position, both facing LOD, step L, scuff, R, scuff

Step L, scuff, R scuff (moving anti-clockwise)	Taking side by side position, facing LOD. Release L hand hold. Step L foot forward.	Scuff R foot next to L foot.	Step R foot forward.	Scuff L foot next to R foot.
	Count 17	**Count 18**	**Count 19**	**Count 20**

Counts 21–28: Release hold, vine L to centre, then R to partner (Partner–vine R to wall then vine L back to partner)

Vine L to centre (moving to centre)	Releasing hold, step L foot to side.	Cross R foot behind L foot.	Step L foot to side.	Hitch R leg and clap hands.
	Count 21	**Count 22**	**Count 23**	**Count 24**
Vine R to partner and wall (moving to wall and partner)	Step R foot to side.	Cross L foot behind R foot.	Step R foot to side.	Hitch L leg, tng to partner and taking double hold.
	Count 25	**Count 26**	**Count 27**	**Count 28**

Begin again.

Ten Step

Couple dance in circle. 18 counts
Music suggestion: Don't Step Out of Line; Go Johnny Go
Choreographer: Unknown

Memory jogger

Begin in side by side position holding L hand to L hand and R hand to R
hand.

Counts 1–4: Dig L, close, tap back R, scuff
Counts 5–10: Dig R, hook, dig, close, dig L, hook
Counts 10–18: Shuffle L, R, L, R

Description with foot patterns

Counts 1–4: Dig L, close, tap back R, scuff

Dig L, close, tap back R, scuff (on the spot)	Dig L heel forward.	Close L foot to R foot.	Tap R foot back.	Scuff R foot next to L foot.
	Count 1	Count 2	Count 3	Count 4

Counts 5–10: Dig R, hook, dig, close, dig L, hook

Dig R, hook, dig, close (on the spot)	Dig R heel forward.	Hook R foot in front of L leg.	Dig R heel forward.	Close R foot to L foot.
	Count 5	Count 6	Count 7	Count 8
Dig L, hook (on the spot)	Dig L heel forward.	Hook L foot in front of R leg.		
	Count 9	Count 10		

Counts 11–18: Shuffle L, R, L, R

Shuffle L (moving forward)	Step L foot forward.	Step R foot towards L foot.	Step L foot forward.
	Count 11	Count &	Count 12
Shuffle R (moving forward)	Step R foot forward.	Step L foot towards R foot.	Step R foot forward.
	Count 13	Count &	Count 14
Shuffle L (moving forward)	Step L foot forward.	Step R foot towards L foot.	Step L foot forward.
	Count 15	Count &	Count 16
Shuffle R (moving forward)	Step R foot forward.	Step L foot towards R foot.	Step R foot forward.
	Count 17	Count &	Count 18

Begin again.

Rebel Strut

Partner dance in circle. 24 counts
Music suggestion: Dancing Boots
Choreographer: Unknown

Memory jogger

Begin in shadow hold, L hand to L hand and R hand to R hand.

Counts 1–4: Dig R, hook, dig, close
Counts 5–12: Dig L, close, point R, close, dig L, close, stomp R, stomp L

Counts 13–16: Pivot turns
Counts 17–24: Shuffles, RLR, LRL, RLR, LRL

Description with foot patterns
Counts 1–4: Dig R, hook, dig, close

Dig R, hook, dig, close *(on the spot)*	Dig R heel forward.	Hook R foot in front of L leg.	Dig R heel forward.	Close R foot to L foot.
	Count 1	**Count 2**	**Count 3**	**Count 4**

Counts 5–12: Dig L, close, point R, close, dig L, close, stomp R, stomp L

Dig L, close, point R, close *(on the spot)*	Dig L foot forward.	Close L foot to R foot.	Tap R toe back.	Close R foot next to L foot.
	Count 5	**Count 6**	**Count 7**	**Count 8**
Dig L, close, stomp R, stomp L *(on the spot)*	Dig L heel forward.	Close L foot to R foot.	Stomp R foot in place.	Stomp L foot in place.
	Count 9	**Count 10**	**Count 11**	**Count 12**

Counts 13–16: Pivot turns

Pivot turns *(tng L)*	Step R foot forward releasing R hands, tng ½ to L under raised L hands.	Replace weight to L foot.	Step R foot forward tng ½ to L. Turn partner under raised L hands.	Replace weight to L foot, rejoining R hands.
	Count 13	**Count 14**	**Count 15**	**Count 16**

Counts 17–24: Shuffles, RLR, LRL, RLR, LRL

Shuffles (moving forward)	Step R foot forward. Count 17	Step L foot towards R foot. Count &	Step R foot forward. Count 18	Step L foot forward. Count 19
	Step R foot towards L foot. Count &	Step L foot forward. Count 20	Step R foot forward. Count 21	Step L foot towards R foot. Count &
	Step R foot forward. Count 22	Step L foot forward. Count 23	Step R foot towards L foot. Count &	Step L foot forward. Count 24

Begin again.

CONCLUSION

There will always be new line dances to learn, thank goodness, so no book of charts can ever be complete. We do hope this book has been of some help to get you started in the easiest and most enjoyable way, and also to persuade you to get out there and give it a try.

Musical suggestions

Do remember these are only our suggestions. Please try other music as well. Love of music goes hand in hand with your love of dance. Variety is the spice of life.

Choreographers

We have tried to make contact with the choreographers mentioned in the book but were not always successful. Every one we did manage to contact gave us lots of help and we heartily thank them. If we didn't reach you, can we please give you our genuine thanks for many happy hours you have given to us and other line dancers.

Useful addresses

We have also tried to contact all those mentioned in the 'Useful Information' section of the book. These, too, have assured all our readers of their help and consideration.

Happy Line Dancing.

GLOSSARY

Below are some explanations of the terms, foot patterns and commonly used figures which may be needed when interpreting dance charts. For ease, they have been arranged in alphabetical order.

Applejack (or Fancy Feet)   Start with the feet a little distance apart. Place the weight on the heel of one foot and the toe of the other foot, for example, the heel of the L foot and the toe of the R foot. Sink into the knees slightly. Spread both toes apart. Straighten the knees and let the toes return to the centre position. Switch the weight putting it on the heel of the R foot and the toe of the L foot. Again sink into the knees slightly. Spread both toes apart. Straighten the knees and let the toes return to the centre position. This needs lots of practice.

Ball change   A change of weight from the ball of one foot to the ball or flat of the other foot. These two movements are usually made on one count.

Brush   A swing of the leg using the hip and knee joint either forward or backward. The moving foot will touch the floor as it passes the supporting foot.

Bumps   A pushing of the hips diagonally forward then backward.

Butterfly or **Buttermilk**   See pigeon toes.

Camel walks   This can also start with weight on L foot stepping forward with R foot.

Begin with weight on R foot	Step L foot forward.	Slide R foot beside L foot taking weight.	Step L foot forward.	Slide R foot beside L foot and touch.
	Count 1	Count 2	Count 3	Count 4

ChaCha shuffles   See shuffles.

Charleston - This can be danced in either of the ways shown. Both versions can be danced on either foot.

Begin with feet together. Weight on L foot	Tap R toe forward in front of L foot (or kick).	Step R foot back.	Tap L toe behind R foot.	Step L foot forward.
	Count 1	Count 2	Count 3	Count 4
Begin with feet together. Weight on L foot	Step L foot forward.	Kick (or tap) R foot forward.	Step R foot back.	Tap L foot back.
	Count 1	Count 2	Count 3	Count 4

Chasses   See shuffles.

Chug walks   These are meant to resemble the action of a train.

Count 1 – Step R foot forward allowing L toes to slide-up to R foot.

Count 2 – Step L foot forward allowing R toes to slide-up to L foot.

The chart will indicate how many chug walks to dance.

Coaster step   This can be performed on either foot.

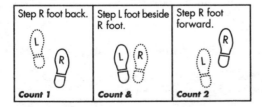

Step R foot back.	Step L foot beside R foot.	Step R foot forward.
Count 1	Count &	Count 2

Coca Rola   See jazz box.

Dig   An emphasised tap made with the heel of the foot without leaving weight.

Double hold   Used in partner dances. Partners face each other with partner's R hand in L hand and partner's L hand in R hand.

Fan   Keeping the heels together, the toes are moved out to the side and then back together again. This can be done with either or both feet.

Flick   This is a brisk movement of the lower leg from the knee in any direction.

Four wall dance   This describes a dance where, at the end of each sequence of steps, you are facing in a different direction. At the end of four sequences you will have faced each wall and be back in your original position.

Grapevine   See vine.

Grapevine (rolling)   See vine (rolling).

Heel clicks or splits   See pigeon toes.

Heel dig   See dig.

Heel fan   See pigeon toes.

Heel raises   Keeping the weight on the R foot, raise L heel and bump R hip to R side. Now raise the R heel and bump L hip to L side. This can be started on either foot.

Heel snap   Raise one or both heels and snap down to the floor using one count for the two movements.

Heel swivels   This can also move to the L.

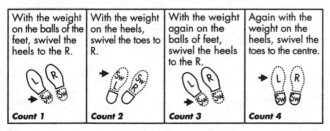

With the weight on the balls of the feet, swivel the heels to the R.	With the weight on the heels, swivel the toes to R.	With the weight again on the balls of feet, swivel the heels to the R.	Again with the weight on the heels, swivel the toes to the centre.
Count 1	*Count 2*	*Count 3*	*Count 4*

Hip bumps   See bumps.

Hip roll   Circle the hips from L to R, or R to L, in a forward or backward motion as instructed.

Hip thrusts   a pelvic movement involving pushing hips forward or backward with a thrusting action.

Hitch   Lifting the leg from the knee. Could also use a hopping action.

Hitch turn   The same as a hitch but also tng to L or R. Both the turn and the hitch are usually performed on one count.

Hold   Hold the body position, pausing for one count.

Hook   Lift the leg from the knee, placing the heel of the L or R foot across the front of or behind the standing leg at shin height. The toe of the unweighted foot should point towards the floor. The term is sometimes used to mean a movement of four counts which incorporates the hook as below.

Hop   To jump forward on one foot and land on the same foot.

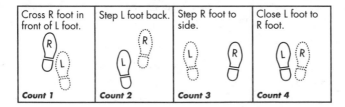

Dig heel forward.	Hook heel across stationary leg.	Dig heel forward.	Close moving foot to stationary foot.
Count 1	Count 2	Count 3	Count 4

In place   The foot is returned to its original position.

Jazz box   There are two variations which may be used. Either version may be danced on either foot and may be turned to L or R.

Variation 1

Cross R foot in front of L foot.	Step L foot back.	Step R foot to side.	Close L foot to R foot.
Count 1	Count 2	Count 3	Count 4

Variation 2

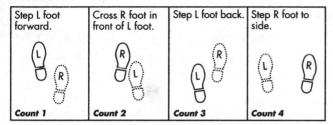

Step L foot forward.	Cross R foot in front of L foot.	Step L foot back.	Step R foot to side.
Count 1	*Count 2*	*Count 3*	*Count 4*

Jumping jack turn   This can also be danced tng to L.

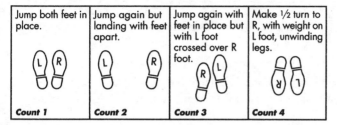

Jump both feet in place.	Jump again but landing with feet apart.	Jump again with feet in place but with L foot crossed over R foot.	Make ½ turn to R, with weight on L foot, unwinding legs.
Count 1	*Count 2*	*Count 3*	*Count 4*

Jumps

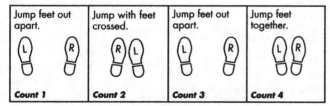

Jump feet out apart.	Jump with feet crossed.	Jump feet out apart.	Jump feet together.
Count 1	*Count 2*	*Count 3*	*Count 4*

Kick   Swing leg out from the hips in any direction.

Kick or flick ball change   The movement can be danced on either foot. It can also be danced in reverse – ball, change kick or flick.

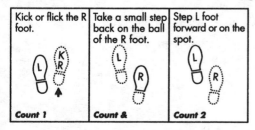

Kick or flick the R foot.	Take a small step back on the ball of the R foot.	Step L foot forward or on the spot.
Count 1	*Count &*	*Count 2*

Kick turn   This is a turn which is made at the same time as kicking.

Knee dip   Lowering the body as the knees are bent.

Lock   Can also be danced moving backward when foot crosses in front.

One foot forward.	The other foot crosses behind.	The first foot moves forward.
L R	L R	L R
Count 1	*Count 2*	*Count 3*

LOD   Refers to 'Line of Dance'. This is the way a normal progression is made around the dance floor in an anti- or counter-clockwise direction. It is mainly used in partner dances.

Lunge   A long step taken in any direction with bent knee. When the step is taken forward, the move is like a fencing lunge.

Military turn   See pivot turn.

Point R foot to side.	Make a ½ turn to R. R foot closes to L foot.	Point L foot to side.	Close L foot to R foot.
L P R	R L	R L	R L
Count 1	*Count 2*	*Count 3*	*Count 4*

Monterey spin or turn   The turn and the close are both made on count two. This can be done using either feet.

One wall dance   Although a dance may have several turns, a one wall dance faces the commencing wall at the end of each full sequence.

Paddle step   This will create a paddling action. The movement can also be danced with L foot and tng to R. Sometimes called a 'Peg leg' turn. Other amounts of turn may also be made.

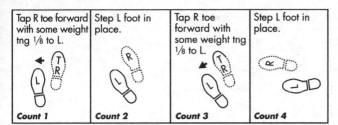

Tap R toe forward with some weight tng 1/8 to L.	Step L foot in place.	Tap R toe forward with some weight tng 1/8 to L.	Step L foot in place.
Count 1	**Count 2**	**Count 3**	**Count 4**

Parallel   This indicates that one foot is held in essentially the same direction as the other foot. 'Parallel' could indicate your normal standing position.

Pigeon toes (or heel splits)   With the weight on the balls of both feet, swing heels apart and back again to their original position, clicking heels together.

Pivot   Count 1: Step R foot forward tng $1/2$ (or $1/4$ or $3/4$) to L. Count 2: Replace full weight forward (or side) to L foot. This can also be made on L foot with the turn being made to the R. The turn is made on the balls of both feet.

Point   Tap toe in the direction stated on the chart without leaving any weight on it.

Reach turns   See switch turn.

Rock step   A step pattern where a rocking motion is performed by transferring body weight from one foot to the other. It can be danced forward, back, side, and across in front or across behind.

Rolling vine   See vine rolling.

Ronde   This is instructing you to move the foot in the shape of an arc. The moving foot could be either on the floor or raised slightly above it.

Sailor step   The three steps are danced on two counts. It can be danced starting with the R foot or crossing in front instead of behind on the first count. It can also be danced with the foot moving to the side on count 2. The swing motion which is caused by this step is meant to be the sailor on board ship.

L foot swings out and behind R foot.	Change weight to R foot.	Change weight to L foot.
R L	R L	L R
Count 1	**Count &**	**Count 2**

Scissors   A four count move: Count 1: Step R foot to side. Count 2: Step L foot next to R foot. Count 3: Step R foot across in front of L foot. Count 4: Hold position. This can also be danced starting with the L foot.

Scoot   This is a hop forward on one foot with the other foot held in a hook position.

Scuff   A moving stamp ending with the foot stretched.

Shadow position   Used in partner dances. Both partners are facing the same way. Partner is slightly more forward. L hand is held in L hand and R hand in R hand unless otherwise stated on the dance chart.

Shimmy   A shaking of the shoulders while dancing any figure.

Shuffles   These are a series of three steps danced in two counts of music. The second step closes, or almost closes, to the first step. For example, Step R foot forward on count 1. L foot almost closes to R foot on count & (see **syncopated rhythm** for explanation of '&'). Step R foot forward on count 2. They can be danced sideways, forwards or backwards and on either foot.

Side by side position   Used in partner dances. Both dancers face the same way with neither of them in advance of the other. a hand is sometimes held.

Skip   This can be danced on either foot.

Step L foot to side.	R foot steps across front of L foot taking weight.	Step L foot to side.
L R	R L	L R
Count 1	**Count &**	**Count 3**

Slap leather   A step which incorporates slapping the sole of either foot with either hand as instructed.

Slide   Sliding one foot to the other while keeping it in light contact with the floor. When the sliding foot reaches the other foot the weight is passed over to it.

Slide-up (or slide without weight)   In a slide-up, the same movement as a slide is performed but the weight remains on the stationary foot.

Spin   A turn made on either foot.

Star   This can be done also on the L foot. It forms half a star shape on the floor.

Tap R foot forward.	Tap R foot to side.	Tap R foot back.	Tap R foot to side.
L · T R	L · T R	L · T R	L · T R
Count 1	**Count 2**	**Count 3**	**Count 4**

Stomp   A short sharp push into the floor by either foot. It is performed with a flexing of the knees.

Stomp-up (or stomp without weight)   As for stomp but without leaving any weight on the foot.

Stroll   This is the same as a vine but travelling diagonally forward.

Strut (heel)   A two count walk stepping on the heel then lowering to the ball of the foot.

Strut (toe)   A two count walk stepping on the toe then lowering to the heel of the foot.

Sugarfoot   First the toe of the R foot is placed to the instep of the L foot. Then the heel of the R foot is placed to the instep of the L foot. This usually takes two counts and can be danced with either foot. Count 3 is usually, though not always, taken across the weighted foot with the position held on count 4.

Swing   A movement where the unweighted foot swings either forwards, sideways or across the body.

Switch   Two moves are performed on one count. Begin with one heel forward. As this foot is brought back in place, the other heel moves forward. A variation to this can be to allow the toes of the other foot to move back as the foot is brought back in place. This can be danced on either foot.

Switch turns   This is danced by tapping R foot forward then making $\frac{1}{2}$ turn to L whilst keeping the weight on the L foot. It can also be danced with L foot tapping forward and tng to R whilst keeping the weight on the R foot.

Swivel   Keeping the toes together, turn heels to L or R and then bring them back into place.

Swivet   Study the foot patterns below. This can then be followed by a similar movement in the opposite direction. These two moves could be reversed by starting with weight on L heel and R toes.

Begin with weight on R heel and L toes.	Swivel R toe to the R and L heel to L.	Swivel R toe to centre and L heel to centre.
	Count 1	**Count 2**

Syncopated rhythm   Most dance steps are choreographed to match full beats of music. On some occasions, steps are choreographed to use half-beats. If this is the case, the count is labelled '&'. For instance, in the counts 1 & 2, this would mean three steps fitting into two counts of music.

Toe taps or touches   The toes can be tapped in any direction. The word 'tap' or 'touch' means that the weight is not transferred.

Triples   See shuffles.

Twinkles   The foot patterns below can be danced with either foot.

Step L foot across R foot.	Step R foot to the R side.	Step L foot in place.
Count 1	**Count &**	**Count 2**

Twist   This instructs you to turn your body without lifting your feet from the floor. The direction of the twist will be specified in the chart. Twists are easier to dance if the knees are bent slightly with the weight taken over the balls of the feet.

Two wall dance   At end of each sequence, you will face the opposite direction from where you started the sequence.

Unwind   This move comes after crossing one foot over the other. If the R foot is crossed, the unwind will be to the L. If L foot is crossed the turn will be to the R. The amount of turn is usually ¹/₂.

Vine   This can refer to either a three or a four step travelling movement usually using one count of music for each step. It can start on either foot and can move to the L or R. In the four step version, the last step may be a stomp, a brush, a scuff, a flick or a variety of movements.

Step L foot to side.	Step R foot behind L foot.	Step L foot to side.	The fourth step varies.
L R	L R	L R	
Count 1	*Count 2*	*Count 3*	*Count 4*

Vine rolling   This is often danced instead of an ordinary vine. A full turn is made over the three counts with the fourth step as above.

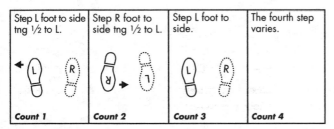

Step L foot to side tng ¹/₂ to L.	Step R foot to side tng ¹/₂ to L.	Step L foot to side.	The fourth step varies.
L R	R → L	L R	
Count 1	*Count 2*	*Count 3*	*Count 4*

Vine with eight counts   The figure can be danced with either foot.

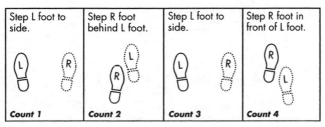

Step L foot to side.	Step R foot behind L foot.	Step L foot to side.	Step R foot in front of L foot.
L R	L R	L R	R L
Count 1	*Count 2*	*Count 3*	*Count 4*

Step L foot to side.	Step R foot behind L foot.	Step L foot to side.	The eighth step varies as with the vine.
Count 5	*Count 6*	*Count 7*	*Count 8*

Weave   This is similar to the eight count vine but in addition it includes vines which are longer than eight counts. It varies from the vine in that it can begin with a crossing step rather than a step to the side.

Without weight   This describes a movement where the weight remains on the stationary foot. It usually means the foot will be used again.

Zig zag   A diagonal step pattern which alternates direction by $^1/_4$ throughout.

FOOT PATTERNS USED IN CHARTS

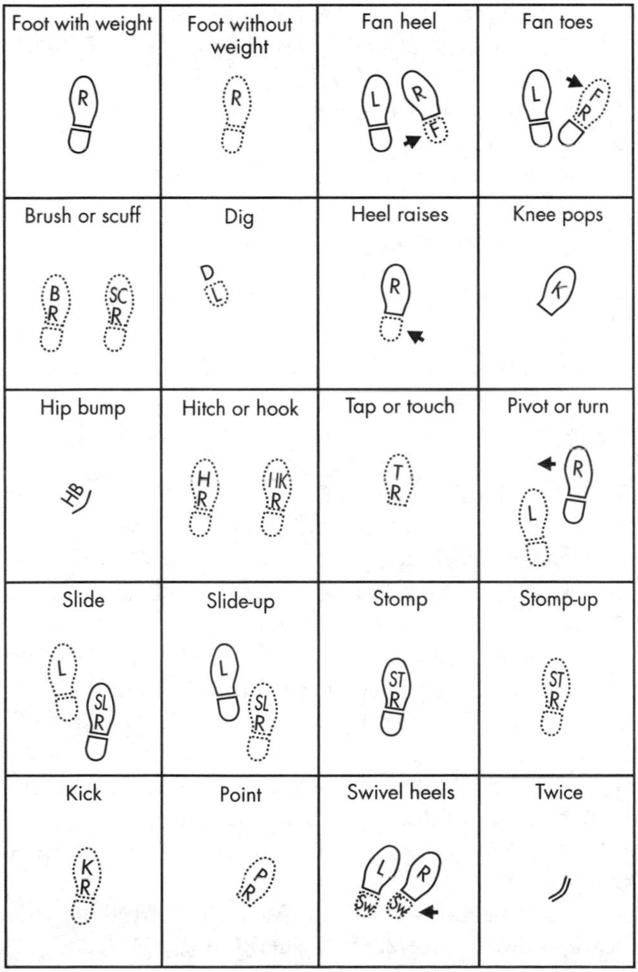
Foot with weight
Foot without weight
Fan heel
Fan toes
Brush or scuff
Dig
Heel raises
Knee pops
Hip bump
Hitch or hook
Tap or touch
Pivot or turn
Slide
Slide-up
Stomp
Stomp-up
Kick
Point
Swivel heels
Twice

DANCE CHARTS WITH MUSIC DETAILS

All Aboard: My Baby Thinks She's a Train by the Dean Brothers.

Alpine: Jackknife, Love to Line Dance 2, Dave Sheriff Stomp DW005.

Black Coffee: Black Coffee by Lacy J Dalton.

Bubba, The: Cleopatra by Pam Tillis; Best of Friends, Western Dance UK, Dave Sheriff TBL 018 CD.

Bus Stop: Dancing Feet, Love to Line Dance 2, Dave Sheriff Stomp DW005.

Cajun Skip: Cajun Strut, Western Dance UK, Dave Sheriff TBL 018 CD.

California Freeze: Oh Johnny, Love to Line Dance 2, Dave Sheriff Stomp DW005.

Canadian Stomp: Hair of the Dog, Love to Line Dance 2, Dave Sheriff Stomp DW005.

Catfish: The Game of Love, Western Dance UK, Dave Sheriff TBL 018 CD.

Charmaine: She's a Little Bit Country, Country Gold Vol II; Whisper Softly, Love to Line Dance 2, Dave Sheriff Stomp DW005.

Chattahoochee: Chattahoochee by Alan Jackson; All Dressed Up, Western Dance UK, Dave Sheriff TBL 018 CD.

Cheyenne: A1 Blues, various arrangements.

Cowboy ChaCha: Because You're Mine by James House; Wish You Were Here, Western Dance UK, Dave Sheriff TBL 018 CD.

Cowboy Motion: Me and My baby, Western Dance UK, Dave Sheriff TBL 018 CD.

Cowboy Rhythm: Cowboy Rhythm, Love to Line Dance, Dave Sheriff Stomp DS007; Baby Likes to Rock It by The Tractors.

Cowboy Strut: And I Worry, Love to Line Dance 2, Dave Sheriff Stomp DW005.

Cowgirls' Twist: What the Cowgirls Do by Vince Gill; Drinking with Both Hands, Love to Line Dance 2, Dave Sheriff Stomp DW005.

Cross My Heart: I Don't Know by the Dean Brothers.

Electric Horseman: Mighty Matador by Dave Sheriff.

Elvira Freeze: Elvira; Drinking with Both Hands, Love to Line Dance 2, Dave Sheriff Stomp DW005.

Flying Eight: Dancing Feet, Love to Line Dance 2, Dave Sheriff Stomp DW005.

Freeze: A1 Blues, Western Dance UK, Dave Sheriff TBL 018 CD.

Fuzzy Duck Slide: Stetson Hat, Love to Line Dance, Dave Sheriff, Stomp DS007.

Grapevine Swing: Heartbeat, Love to Line Dance 2, Dave Sheriff Stomp DW005.

Grundy Gallop: Sold by John Michael Montgomery; Heart Made of Stone, Love to Line Dance 2, Dave Sheriff Stomp DW005.

Hardwood Stomp: Heartbeat, Love to Line Dance 2, Dave Sheriff Stomp DW005. Hardwood Stomp, Rick Tippe, Dance On.

Heads or Tails: Heads Carolina, Tails California by Jo Dee Messina.

Honky Tonk Stomp: The Sun Don't Shine on Me, Western Dance UK, Dave Sheriff TBL 018 CD.

Honky Tonk Twist II: Twisting the Night Away by Scooter Lee.

Hooked on Country: Hooked on Country Part 1 by Atlanta Pops Orchestra; And I Worry, Love to Line Dance 2, Dave Sheriff Stomp DW005.

Houston Slide: Backtrack, Love to Line Dance 2, Dave Sheriff Stomp DW005.

I Love You Too: I Love You Too, Western Dance UK, Dave Sheriff TBL 018 CD.

Kensas City Stomp: Dancing Boots, Western Dance UK, Dave Sheriff TBL 018 CD.

Little Sister: Stetson Hat, Love to Line Dance 2, Dave Sheriff Stomp DW005.

One Step Forward: One Step Forward by Desert Rose Band; Go Johnny Go, Western Dance UK, Dave Sheriff TBL 018 CD.

Queen of Memphis: Queen of Memphis by the Dean Brothers; The Sun Don't Shine on Me, Western Dance UK, Dave Sheriff TBL 018 CD.

Rebel Strut: Dancing Boots, Western Dance UK, Dave Sheriff TBL 018 CD.

Reggae Cowboy: Reggae Cowboy by The Bellamy Brothers.

Ribbon of Highway: Ribbon of Highway by Scooter Lee.

Running Bear: Running Bear by the Dean Brothers.

Ski Bumpus: Modification, Love to Line Dance 2, Dave Sheriff Stomp DW005.

State Line Waltz: (Who Says) You Can't Have It All by Alan Jackson; More Than One Heart, Western Dance UK, Dave Sheriff TBL 018 CD.

Stroll Along ChaCha: Big Hair by The Bellamy Brothers; Stroll Along, Love to Line Dance, Dave Sheriff Stomp DS007.

Ten Step: Don't Step Out of Line, Country Line Dancing CD; Go Johnny Go, Western Dance UK, Dave Sheriff TBL 018 CD.

Tennessee Stroll: Me and My Baby, Western Dance UK, Dave Sheriff TBL 018 CD.

Texan Boogie: A1 Blues, Western Dance UK, Dave Sheriff TBL 018 CD.

Texas Stomp: Down on the Farm by Tim McGraw.

Tush Push: Backtrack, Love to Line Dance 2, Dave Sheriff Stomp DW005.

Western Barn Dance: Rock My World, Absolute Country CD; Western Express, Western Dance UK, Dave Sheriff TBL 018 CD.

Wrangler Butts: Wrangler Butts by Jeff Moore from Fever 3.

USEFUL ADDRESSES

Country and Western Dancing Organisations

All Ireland Board of Ballroom Dancing
George Devlin
Pine Ridge
Kilmacanogue
Co Wicklow
Ireland
Tel: 00 353 1 286 8101

Allegemeiner Deutscher Tanziehrer Verband
President: Heiko Feltens
Monchengang 7–9
Dortmund
D-44135
Germany
Tel: 00 49 231 524 444

Allied Dancing Association Ltd
Secretary: Edna Murphy
71 Haileybury Road
Woolton
Liverpool
L25 8SN
Tel: 0151 428 1312

Association Espanola de Professores de Bailes de Salon
President: Ferran Rovira
Gran de Gracia 51
08012 Barcelona
Spain
Tel: 00 343 218 38 17

Australian Dancing Board
Secretary: Derek Gatley
49 Links Road
Ardross 6153
Western Australia
Tel: 00 61 9 364 3553

British Western Dance Association
Oasis Dance Centre
Unit 1
North Works
Watery Lane
Preston
PR2 1QJ
Tel: 01772 734324

**Canadian Dance
Teachers' Association**
Mrs P Nikleva
8160 Lucas Rd
Richmond V6Y 1G3
Canada
Tel: 00 1 604 277 6480

China Sport Dance Association
Mrs Wang Wei Jian
No 54 Bashiqiao Rd
Haidian District
Beijing 100044
China
Tel: 00 86 10 6833 8518

**Conseil Français Prof. de
Danse Social**
President: René Barsi
22 Rue Victor Hugo
Montreuil 93100
France
Tel: 00 33 1 48 592 124

**Consiglio Italiano
Dansa Sportiva**
Walter Santinelli
Via delle Medaglie Oro 49
00136 Roma
Italy
Tel: 00 396 397 2891

**Country Western Dance
Council (UK)**
Secretary: R W Cooper
8 Wick Lane
Felpham
Bognor Regis
West Sussex
PO22 8QG

CPDA
President: Elio Basan
Veruda 22
Pula 52000
Croatia
Tel: 00 385 52 517 083

DOF
President: Jorgen Christensen
Fredericksvaerkgade 43a
3400 Hillerod
Denmark
Tel: 00 45 4226 5709/45

**Guild of Professional Teachers of
Dancing and Movement to Music**
Secretary: N Yates
16 Cherry Tree Road
Moreton
Wirral
L46 9RF
Tel: 0151 677 8498

**Hong Kong Ballroom
Dancing Council**
President: Walter Wat
10 Jubilee Street
5/F Room 502 Central
Hong Kong
Tel: 00 852 2541 6215

**Imperial Society of Teachers
of Dancing**
Euston Hall
Birkenhead Street
London
WC1H 8BE
Tel: 0171 837 9967

**International Dance
Teachers' Association**
76 Bennetts Lane
Brighton
BN2 5JL
Tel: 01 273 685 652

**Israel Association of Teachers
and Professional Dancers**
President: Anatoli Trilisky
POB 6139
Kiryat Eqron 70500
Israel
Tel: 00 972 8 941 1476

Japan Dance Council
Edward Kibata
1888-4 Minami-Kaname
Hiratsuka City
Kanagawa-Pref 259-12
Japan
Tel: 00 81 463 58 8847

Malaysian Dancers' Association
President: Dr Henry Ooi
Kwee Lim
119 York Road
10450 Penang
Tel: 00 604 261 5497

**Malta Dance and Dance
Sport Council**
Chairman: Louis Baldacchino
Peacock Buildings
No 101 Testaferrata Street
Msida MSD02
Malta
Tel: 00 356 310146

**National Dance Council
of America**
President: Brian McDonald
24556 Mando Drive
Laguna
Niguel
California CA 92677
USA
Tel: 00 1 714 643 9700

**National Dance Council
of Greece**
President: Socrates Charos
80 Kareas Avenue
Bironas 16233
Greece
Tel: 00 301 764 2173/301

**Nederlanse Bond van
Dansleraren**
Secretary: Fred Bijster
JB weg 6
7991 RG Dwingeloo
Holland
Tel: 00 31 52159 2071

Norges Danselaerer-Forbund
President: Svein Rotvold
Kartsveien 178
2013 Skjetten
Norway
Tel: 00 47 63 842228

**Northern Counties Dance
Teachers' Association Ltd**
Secretary: Linda Dudman
67 Elizabeth Drive
Palmersville
Newcastle upon Tyne
NE12 9QP
Tel: 0191 268 2372

Professional Dance Teachers' Association of the Philippines
President: Douglas Nierras
3/F Bo. Kapitolyo
Pasig City 1603
Philippines
Tel: 00 63 2 631 6489

Russian Dance Union
President: Stanislav Popov
Novatorov Str 26–52
117421 Moscow
Russia
Tel: 00 7 095 432 3229

Singapore Ballroom Dance Teachers' Association
President: Sunny Low
263 Outram Rd
Singapore 0316
Tel: 00 65 276 1015/65

Thailand Association of Teachers of Dancing
President: Burin Wongsanguan
4/Floor Peninsula Plaza RM 401
153 Rajdamri Road
Lumpini
Bangkok 10330
Thailand
Tel: 00 662 251 7816/662

Ukrainian Dance Board
Chairman: Miss Irena Bous
26–13 Pancha Street
L LVIV 290020
Ukraine
Tel: 00 380 322 330 608

United Kingdom Alliance
386–392 Lytham Road
Blackpool
FY4 1DW
Tel: 01 253 408 828

Yugoslav Dance Teachers' Association
President: Zorica Lukic
11000 Belgrade Viktoria
Igoe 4
Yugoslav
Tel: 00 381 11 412 427

Country and Western Dancing Publications

American Line & Western Dancer Magazine
Oasis Dance Centre
Watery Lane
Preston
PR2 1QJ
Tel: 01772 734324

International Dance Magazine
Editor Malcolm J Owen
3 Church Road
East Huntspill
Somerset
TA9 3PG
Tel: 01278 792233

Linedancer Magazine
Publisher Betty Drummond
Clare House
166 Lord Street
Southport
PR9 0QA
Tel: 01704 501235

On Line Linedancing Magazine
Editor Rob O'Brian
The Church Hall
Church Crescent
Coedkernew
Newport
NP1 9TT
Tel: 01633 680 494

Dave Sheriff News Club
PO Box 427
Tweedale
Telford
Shropshire
TF3 1WA
Tel: 01952 270711

Line Dance UK!
Editor Mick Green
Published by Pebble View
Publishing Ltd
8 Pebble View Walk
Hopton-on-Sea
Norfolk
NR31 9SG
Tel: 01502 732040

North Country Music & Line Dancing
455 Alfreton Road
Nottingham
NG7 5LX
Tel: 0115 9422 615

Pathfinder
J W Brookfield
128 Bedford Road
Southport
PR8 4HP
Tel: 01704 569441

TEACH YOURSELF

Ballroom Dancing
The Imperial Society of Teachers of Dancing

Have you ever wished you could waltz confidently around the dance floor with a partner? With this book to guide you, you need never make a false step again.

Written with the absolute beginner in mind, this book deals with all aspects of dancing for social occasions in a clear and practical style. All the most popular dances are explained step by step with thorough instruction for both partners, as well as a variety of Latin American and current trend dances and steps suitable for disco/freestyle dancing.

TEACH YOURSELF

Tai Chi

Robert Parry

Tai chi is a centuries-old system of exercise from China which is gaining increasing popularity in the West. The movements flow into one another in a slow, graceful pattern and are suitable for all ages and levels of fitness.

This richly illustrated book explains the basics of tai chi and contains step-by-step instructions for learning the Short Yang Form – a sequence of gentle exercise that takes only eight minutes to complete. Daily practice promotes relaxation and well-being and increases levels of concentration and personal creativity. Tai chi is the prefect antidote to the stressful life of today.

Robert Parry has a life-long interest in the health and relaxation aspects of Eastern systems of exercise. He is a qualified shiatsu practitioner and an experienced teacher of tai chi.

[ty] TEACH YOURSELF

Yoga

Mary Stewart

Teach yourself Yoga explains yoga breathing and meditation with clear step-by-step instructions and illustrations showing you how to perform the poses. The book also includes a basic beginner's sequence to help you establish a daily practice routine.

Yoga postures and breathing promote flexibility and strength, relieve the stress of every day living and bring peace of mind. With regular practice and application this ancient system can transform your life.

Mary Stewart has been teaching yoga for over thirty years. She is the author of five books on the subject, including one for children, and has students still practising in their eighties.

The Music for the Dance
On CD or Cassette

*From the popular
Line Dance Songwriter*

Dave Sheriff

74 songs covering OVER 100 DANCES
(including all the dances that you have
learnt in this book) on 5 ALBUMS

DDS 002 Western Dance UK
DS 003 New Western Dance
DS 004 Love to Line Dance 1
DS 005 Love to Line Dance 2
DS 007 Love to Line Dance 3
CDs £12 Cassettes £7
(Including P & P)

--✂--

SAVE £10! – ALL 5 CDs FOR £50
(5 Cassettes for £25)

Name ....

Address ....

.... Postcode ....

Cut & Mail to: Stomp Music PO Box 427 Tweedale TF3 1WA UK
Tel +44(0) 1952 2707111 Fax 413691 www.stompmusic.co.uk